Second Image

This book is dedicated to a dark-eyed girl who once sang chansons in a Québec dancehall, and with affection and gratitude to all my graduate students at l'Université de Sherbrooke, who had the courage to undertake a novel experiment in transcending the cultural barriers of Canada.

second image

Comparative Studies in Québec/Canadian Literature

RONALD SUTHERLAND

New Press / Toronto 1971

ISBN 0-88770-047-0 cloth

Design/Peter Maher

Photo credits/Miller Services, Toronto/Pridham's Studio, Amherst, N.S.

Printed and bound in Canada by The Alger Press Ltd., Oshawa
new press
84 Sussex Avenue
Toronto 179

300 West Adams
Chicago, Illinois, 60606, U.S.A.

CONTENTS

Introduction

My interest in Comparative Canadian Literature began on a Saturday night, in a dancehall on the outskirts of a small Québec town. With the others in the hall I was relaxing after three or four square-dance sets, while an attractive dark-eyed girl entertained us with French-Canadian *chansons*. As I recall, she had a soft, hypnotic voice, and I was listening passively without really paying a great deal of attention, until suddenly I recognized the tune of one of her songs. It was unmistakable—the old Scottish favorite called "Mrs. MacLeod of Raasay," familiar to anyone who has heard an eightsome reel in Canada, Scotland or elsewhere. Completely unfamiliar to me, however, were the words, sounds and gestures which the girl was using to interpret this lively melody.

When she had finished her performance, I made a point of talking to her. I asked her about the song, and she replied without the slightest hesitation that it was a very old, traditional French-Canadian *chant folklorique*!

"Etes-vous absolument certaine?" I continued.

"Mais oui," she said, "absolument. Je l'ai apris de ma grand'maman."

And a warm summer night with good music, cold drinks and pretty girls in the mood to dance is no time for an argument.

But afterwards I thought about the girl's remark. I began to wonder about the things the cultures of French and English Canada have in common, things often undocumented, more often unnoticed, very often unconscious. And in recent years, too often frantically denied.

Nothing came of my speculations for a time. Then I found myself head of a proposed department of English Language and Literature at the new Université de Sherbrooke, and the speculations burst forth anew. At Sherbrooke, unhindered by long established academic traditions, or at least partly removed from their conditioning force, my colleagues and I decided to go out on a limb. Arguing—for we were not without strong opposition at the beginning—that standard departments of English were quite secure, there being at least one in each Canadian college or university, we proposed the creation of a programme of studies leading to the novel and unique degree of Master of Arts in Comparative Canadian Literature. Now that I think back to 1962 when the programme began to take shape, I have the deepest admiration for those students who embarked upon this unorthodox pattern of studies. They must have had remarkable courage and confidence, for attitudes being what they usually are in arts faculties, there was considerable academic risk. After all, even now there are some universities in Canada which have not as yet accepted Canadian Literature, French or English, as appropriate subject matter for even a course, let alone a degree.

Fortunately, all has gone well. Graduates with the

Master of Arts in Comparative Canadian Literature are now at large, teaching, continuing their studies, writing and beginning to publish. And the programme continues to grow and mature.

The essays included in this volume are the by-products of my experimental seminars in Comparative Canadian Literature. To prepare for these seminars I and my students simply read a large number of books by English-Canadian and French-Canadian writers. Then we met and talked, tossing ideas and interpretations back and forth. Gradually, however, certain unifying or transcendent themes and patterns seemed to become evident, and they were tested by reading more books. The most significant of these themes and patterns are what the essays in this volume are about. Stated simply then, Comparative Canadian Literature is the application of literary analysis to the works of Canadian writers, regardless of whether these works are in English or in French. It is literary criticism informed by knowledge, and by a desire for more knowledge of essential aspects of Canadian Literature as a whole. Its purpose, therefore, is to determine through broadened view and comparison the interlocking themes, the common insights, the merits and the weaknesses of creative writing produced by members of the two major ethnic groups of Canada.

Comparative Literature, of course, has long been a standard and respected discipline in academic communities throughout the world. All of the great literary scholars have to some extent been comparatists, for greatness depends upon a breadth as well as a depth of vision. Comparative Literature has expanded and flourished as a discipline because it has been an instrument to distinguish the universally significant from the parochial and provincial. And in so doing, it has also increased the comprehension and heightened the awareness of what is important in particular national literatures. It has permitted an examination of the inter-influences among different cultural traditions, and such inter-influences, as we know, have been the crucial factors in the whole cultural evolution of man. The field of comparative studies has always been enriched by the art of translation, and translation in turn has been inspired by comparative studies.

Comparative Literature not only improves our understanding of other literatures but also of our own, perhaps especially of our own. For it is an approach which provides perspective, standards of judgement and tested norms. So far as Canadian Literature is concerned, the comparative approach has two distinct aspects. First, Canadian Literature in general can be compared with the literatures of other countries. Secondly, Canadian Literature in French can be compared with Canadian Literature in English. It is to this second aspect that I primarily refer when I use the term Comparative Canadian Literature, although in practice the study of Comparative Canadian Literature often spills over into general Comparative Literature. In particular, there are illuminating comparisons to be made between Canadian Literature and American Literature, and I strongly suspect that similarly fertile possibilities exist with respect to the literatures of Russia, of the nations of South America and Africa, and perhaps of Australia and New Zealand. In Canada itself, creative works in languages other than English and French, in Ukrainian or Gaelic for example, invite comparative analysis. In short, there is no reason why the study of Comparative Canadian Literature should not transcend its own boundaries when inviting prospects come to light. Strictly within the defined boundaries, however, there is a great deal of virgin territory still to explore. And if in terms of literary understanding the general field of Comparative Literature has obvious and undisputed justification, then Comparative Canadian Literature has no less. Moreover, for Canadians of both major languages it holds the additional, para-literary promise of an increase in understanding—of each group by members of the other group as well as by its own members, and of the common mystique shared by all.

I never have managed to unravel the mystery of "Mrs. MacLeod of Raasay." Was the tune transmitted to Québec folk music when the Fraser Highlanders were disbanded here and took French-Canadian wives some two hundred years ago? Does it perhaps go further back to the ancestral lands of Normandy and Brittany? We know how extensive the cultural contacts were between Scotland and France, and the tune may well have come to French-speaking Québec by two routes, indirectly through the Scots immigrants and directly through the French. But I am content to leave this particular problem in the capable hands of Professor Luc Lacourcière, whose Canadian Studies School at Laval University continues to do valuable research in Canadian folklore. The more formal literary products of English and French Canada, increasing now at a tremendous rate, provide more than ample material to occupy my attention. The essays in this book are presented in the hope that these products, in concert as well as separately, will soon occupy the attention of many others.

NOTE ON TEXT PRESENTATION

All page references in this volume are to the editions listed in the Bibliography.

With a view to preserving as much as possible the full flavour of quotations from works in French, while at the same time not requiring the reader to be bilingual, I have adopted a two-sided policy. Single lines and short passages not likely to be misunderstood by anyone with a knowledge of school French are left in the original. Long passages and expressions in colloquial diction or otherwise likely to present problems for those who are not fluent in French, are given in my own translation. Since my translations are not literal, but attempts to capture the spirit of the originals, I have retained the French texts in the footnotes.

Twin Solitudes

"One of the functions and responsibilities of literature,"
says the American critic Marius Bewley, "is to define
nationality in the act of describing or dramatizing it."
And when one considers French literature, American
literature, English literature, indeed any of the distinctive national literatures, it is clear that Bewley's
statement is correct. These literatures have accomplished the subtle definition of nationality. However
intricate and mysterious the process of recognition,
citizens of the various nations are somehow able to
recognize themselves as such. Language, philosophy,
theology, history, politics, and a variety of other things
undoubtedly make their contribution, but in the final
analysis it is literature which has up to now provided
the definition. Key writers, either consciously
or unconsciously, have created their works within particular mystiques. Which is not to say, incidentally, that
these works are necessarily regional, or chauvinistic, or

even lacking in universal significance, but simply that they have been distilled through the complex apparatus of national myth and national sense of identity. One thinks of Shakespeare, Mark Twain, Chekhov, Molière or Robert Burns.

Then one thinks of Canada and Canadian literature; and a number of somewhat troubling speculations come immediately to mind.

What about Canadian literature? Has it succeeded in even suggesting a definition of Canadian identity? If so, what are the aspects of this definition? If not, is it because of a weakness in the literature? Have the key writers not yet emerged? Have they gone unnoticed? Or could it be that there is no distilling apparatus of positive Canadian myth and sense of identity adequate to condition our creative writers? Supposing such an absence, is it detrimental to the creative process? Moreover, and what is probably the most vital question of all, in a country with two distinct languages and literary traditions, neither one manifestly dominant over the other in terms of production or quality, each one apparently isolated from the other, are we to presume two independent definitions of the same sense of identity, or rather two separate national mystiques each with its separate definition; or, in line with certain pessimistic comments of the last few years, would we be wise to presume nothing at all?

This essay will be an attempt, through parallel analyses of principal themes in the twentieth-century French-Canadian and English-Canadian novel, to shed some light upon these questions. It does not, of course, intend to provide conclusive answers to all or any of the questions posed, but is conceived rather as a prolegomenon to further study.

Of the thousands of novels which have been written in French and English Canada, there are only a few, it would seem, which have had any kind of impact on any segment of the national consciousness. For particular attention in this essay, I have selected those novels which seem to me to be the most appropriate for the socio-literary study proposed, but I have also tried to select from among those works which have lasting artistic and thematic qualities.

As the Introduction to this volume explains, until now very little has been attempted in the area of comparative Canadian literature. Yet when placed side by side, each of the literary traditions of Canada becomes far more meaningful than when considered apart. And if I may submit a conclusion before I have properly begun, when French-Canadian and English-Canadian novels are examined together, it becomes evident that there are many significant parallels, parallels which loom all the more fascinating as one discovers the improbability of inter-influence. It also becomes evident, interestingly enough, that a good number of the accepted differences between the cultures of French Canada and English Canada do not in fact exist. For both English-speaking and French-speaking Canadians, major writers included, are guilty of taking a small segment of the other society, albeit shaped into mythic reality, and using it as a substitute for the complex whole.

Both the French-Canadian and the English-Canadian novel have gone through a remarkable evolution in the last forty years or so. During this evolution, three major interlocking themes have emerged:

1 The Land and Divine Order;
2 The Breakup of the Old Order;
3 The Search for Vital Truth.

In the literature of French Canada, the first of these major themes—"Land and Divine Order"—is illustrated by what has been called *le roman paysan* or *le roman du*

4

terroir. Louis Hémon's popular *Maria Chapdelaine*, of course, is the best known of this group of novels and has undoubtedly had the greatest influence. The climax of the tradition came in the late thirties with the publication of Félix-Antoine Savard's *Menaud maître-draveur* and Ringuet's *Trente Arpents*. *Menaud maître-draveur*, which reproduces passages from *Maria Chapdelaine* throughout its text, is not of the same stature as either Hémon's or Ringuet's work. In a way it resembles Ralph Connor's *The Man from Glengarry*, although it falls far short of the latter in convincing description of the river drives. It has none of the detail characteristic of Connor, such as the loggers all standing around attentively, waiting for the telltale snap as MacDonald Mhor bends a man over his knee, about to break his back. On the other hand, it does not degenerate into a Sunday School tract, as does Connor's book. Nobody, including his adored daughter, converts Menaud into a lover of all men. He remains a psychopath, obsessed with the idea of the "the enemy." In Savard's work there is a certain originality of style, incorporating Canadianisms into the prose in a manner which perhaps foreshadows the stylistic experiments of a few very recent French-Canadian novels, experiments which we shall consider later; but *Menaud maître-draveur* is a prose poem rather than a realistic novel. Viewed as a prose poem, its sentimentality, subjectivity and distortion are less detrimental to the value of the work. *Maria Chapdelaine* and *Trente Arpents*, on the other hand, are realistic novels of high merit and penetrating insight.

It has been recognized for years that Louis Hémon succeeded in crystallizing fundamental values of French-Canadian rural society through the characters in the novel *Maria Chapdelaine*. There is a kind of masochism in the father of the family, who will not allow himself to remain on a farm once he has brought it to the point of productivity, but must move again into the wilderness, dragging his family along with him. The mother Chapdelaine, who has always secretly yearned for an easier life, remains loyal to the end, when wasted from years of toil and deprivation she gives up and dies. Just before her death, which the father obviously finds more annoying than tragic, he tries to cheer her up by saying: "You will die when the good Lord wants you to die, and I don't figure it's time yet. What would he do with you? Heaven is full of old ladies, but here we've got only one, and she can still do a little work, sometimes."[1]

Maria will be like her mother. She has moments of doubt, especially in connection with the handsome adventurer François Paradis. When he is lost in the bush, she takes the appropriate measures. She knows that if one repeats a thousand *Ave Marias* on the day before Christmas, and asks a favour of God, then barring extraordinary designs on the part of the divinity, the favour will be granted. Unfortunately, it appears that God does have extraordinary designs in this particular instance, and François freezes to death in the forest. At first, it is hard for Maria to accept. "Christ Jesus, who hold out your arms to the unfortunate," she says to herself, "why didn't you deliver him from the snow with your pale hands? Why, Holy Virgin, didn't you permit a small miracle when he stumbled for the last time? In all the heavenly legions, why couldn't he have had an angel to show him the way?"[2] But Maria's doubts do not last long, for like her father and mother she knows the deep satisfaction of being sure. As Hémon put it: "Oh! Certainty! The contentment of an august promise which dispels the terrible fog of death. While the priest was performing the holy rites and his murmur mixed with the sighs of the dying woman, Samuel Chapdelaine and his children prayed without lifting their heads, almost consoled, free from doubt and worry, certain that whatever happened was according to a pact with the divinity, which made the blue heaven sown with stars of gold an authentic blessing."[3] Maria, then, can turn down the offer of Lorenzo Surprenant to go with him to the United States, and accept a continuation of her mother's life by marrying her neighbour Eutrope Gagnon.

Throughout the novel *Maria Chapdelaine*, one is always aware of the two major thematic ideas, the land and the divine order. In fact, these ideas merge into one, for the land, with its changeless cycle of seasons, its absolute permanence, its mixture of cruel severity and arbitrary sustenance, becomes symbolic of the accepted divine order. The more a person is in harmony with the land, therefore, the more he is in harmony with God. Or perhaps I should say with a particular concept of God, considering the stern, unremitting nature of the land in question—the Jansenist, Calvinist, Puritan concept of God.

Turning to Frederick Philip Grove's *Our Daily Bread* and Ringuet's *Trente Arpents*, one finds the same thematic ideas of the land and the divine order, although both books also introduce the beginning of the dissolution of the old order. As a matter of fact, *Our Daily Bread* and *Trente Arpents*, the first published in 1928 and the second in 1938, are so strikingly similar in theme and plot and even in certain scenes that one wonders if Philippe Panneton had ever read Grove. On the other hand, the two books are entirely different in detail, in atmosphere, in technique, so that in the highly unlikely event that Ringuet did borrow certain ideas he subjected them thoroughly to his own creative process. *Trente Arpents*, it must be pointed out, is a far better novel than *Our Daily Bread*. Its rhythmic prose, its skilful use of colloquial diction, an accurate representation of French-Canadian *joual*, is vigorous and captivating, in contrast to Grove's stiff, often lumbering style. Ringuet had a genius for selecting the kind of small detail which brings a character alive, engaging the imagination and sympathy of the reader. When Phydime Raymond, for example, visits Euchariste Moisan to negotiate for Moisan's half of a small wood, which he desperately wishes to buy, the ancestral Norman propensity for circumlocution is illustrated in a manner worthy of Maupassant at his best. Raymond explains that he has come to see if the sick cow is getting better. Then the conversation, between drags on their pipes, proceeds to diseases in general, the weather, the icy road which is becoming dangerous, the elections. On his way out the door, Raymond inquires about the fence bordering the two properties and who should repair it that year. Then he, who is the one wanting to buy Moisan's half of the wood, offers to sell his half to Moisan, observing that it isn't worth ten dollars to him. And Moisan, who has not the least notion of buying land, says that such a purchase might be a good idea. And on they go, each somehow divining exactly what the other has in mind. Compared to Ringuet's technique of characterization, Grove's is stark and clinical. Nonetheless, considered as an artistic whole, despite its obvious shortcomings, *Our Daily Bread* does make a deep impression upon the reader, an impression of magnitude of vision. It may well have as permanent a place in Canadian literature as *Trente Arpents*.

The parallels in the two novels are manifest. Both stories concern a man obsessed with the idea of building a dynasty upon the land, an Old-Testament type of dynasty. Both men, Euchariste Moisan and John Elliot, have loyal, long-suffering wives, each of whom was chosen to bear children and each of whom brings four sons and six daughters into the world. Alphonsine, Moisan's wife, dies delivering her last child, while Martha Elliot is a victim of cancer of the womb, making them both martyrs to their husbands' obsessions. Like Chapdelaine's wife and Alphonsine, Martha has always secretly harboured a sense of frustration, but she is the only one of the three who gets a chance to express this long denied feeling. In a fantastic scene, perhaps one of Grove's best, she rises from her deathbed and goes to a dance, the loose, heavy folds of her dress draping grotesquely about her wasted body.

Samuel Chapdelaine, John Elliot and Euchariste Moisan have identical attitudes toward the land. Elliot's daughter Cathleen, the only one who makes a successful marriage, chooses a university professor. Of this man Elliot speculates: "Woodrow Ormond, a sensible man, mature beyond his years! But unanchored in the soil. (p. 11) In *Trente Arpents*, speaking of the "habitant" farm establishments, Ringuet wrote: "La patrie c'est la terre, et non le sang." (p. 59) The land is more important than even the blood. And coping with the land isolates the Elliots, the Moisans and the Chapdelaines from even the most monumental events of the outside world. Hearing of the prospects for World War I, Moisan is completely baffled: "Those people," he says, "how can they think about fighting when the harvest isn't in yet." He begins to see how war fits into the divine order when the local priest explains to him: "La France sera punie; elle a chassé les prêtres." (p. 151) When John Elliot discovers that his own son Arthur has joined up, his reaction is "Enlisted? What were we coming to? Meddling in the European war?" (p. 236) At the end of *Our Daily Bread*, Elliot staggers across miles of country, finally crawls the last few yards on his hands and knees, to die on his own piece of land. At the end of *Trente Arpents*, Moisan is still alive, working as a watchman in an American garage and dreaming of his thirty acres, but earlier in the book there is a scene similar to the climax of *Our Daily Bread*. Ephrem Moisan, the uncle from whom Euchariste inherited his farm, is found lying on one of his fields: "Il était mort sur sa terre, poitrine contre poitrine, sur sa terre qui n'avait pas consenti au divorce" (p. 36)—breast against breast, on his land, which had not consented to a divorce.

Moisan and Elliot are both denied the realization of their dreams. Elliot witnesses the complete disintegration of his tiny empire, Moisan is dispossessed by his son Etienne, and as old men they are both helpless and unwanted, compelled to visit children in surroundings which are alien and incomprehensible. Elliot is a sad misfit in his daughter's elegant Winnipeg home, and old Moisan wanders aimlessly around the American town where his son Ephrem has settled. Not one of their many children adopts the values of the father.

It is perhaps Grove who best sums up these values when he has John Elliot say, "I don't want my children and sons-in-law to be rich. But I want them to show me to my satisfaction that they can make their daily bread." (p. 217) In other words, the purpose of life is not the pursuit of comfort or happiness according to one's lights, but to fit into the design conditioned by the land, to fit into the divine order. Happiness does not enter the picture, no more for John Elliot than for Samuel Chapdelaine or Euchariste Moisan. As Jean Simard put it in *Mon Fils pourtant heureux*: "On y est pour faire son devoir, voilà tout. La vie n'est pas un roman." (p. 60) When Elliot rationalizes with the words, "If God had ordained things that way, perhaps there was a meaning to it, a purpose" (p. 60), he professes the same almost masochistic resignation as the Chapdelaines, the same *"acte de soumission à la volonté divine"* as found in *Trente Arpents*.

There is no need to look further than these three novels for clarification of the first major theme. The philosophy of life concerned is clear. It is one which could induce a strong power of endurance, a sense of absolute security. Man in harmony with the cycles of nature, with the noble calling of the land, with the

divine order. Man constantly reminded of his subor-
dinate status by the caprices of nature, yet assured by
this very subordination of a complementary superior
force, a Providence, a greater design of which he is a
part. There is no need to search for meaning. Within the
framework, the human cycle of birth, marriage, death is
simple, sufficient and all-meaning.

The conclusion one must come to after considering
the observations of these three writers is that rural
French Canada and rural English Canada shared the
same fundamental values. Despite differences of
language, religion and degree of involvement with an
organized church, the basic view of man and the land, as
detected by three novelists who made a point of
analyzing this view, was the same across Canada, and
perhaps throughout the Western World for that matter.
One suspects, however, that there is a peculiarly
Canadian flavour in the determination to embrace a life
whose requirements presuppose a sacrifice. Perhaps it
has something to do with the inhospitality of the
land and the severity of the climate. Perhaps it is related
to the spectre of defeat inherited by French Canadians
and English Canadians alike. For it is often forgotten in
French Canada that the founders of so-called English
Canada—the United Empire Loyalists, the Scottish
Highlanders, the Irish and Ukrainians—can hardly be
said to have settled here on the wave of victory.

The second major thematic idea which emerges from
a comparative study of the French-Canadian and
English-Canadian novel—"Breakup of the Old Order"—
can be observed in a large number of novels, including
the final sections of *Our Daily Bread* and *Trente
Arpents*. In other words, many writers have attempted
and are still attempting to analyze the transitional
period and the process by which one set of values is
replaced by another. The culmination of this process
coincides with large scale urbanization, man's removal

from dependence upon the cycles of nature, but it would not be correct to label the contrasting values as rural and urban in application. The new values have spread into rural areas, just as the old values for a long time generally held true for people in cities. As Harvey Cox shrewdly theorizes in *The Secular City*, the whole evolution of modern values began two thousand years ago when Christianity replaced the ancient and isolating tribal deities and the equally isolating city-state deities by a supposedly unifying, universal concept. It has just taken a long time for the implications of this concept to sink in. The older ideas, including those governing man's relationship to the land and nature, have hung on in new guises, Christian guises; and those least willing to accept the implications of the new concept, or least able to understand them, have more often than not been the authorities of the Christian Church itself.

In the second group of novels, harmony with the divine order is replaced by the pursuit of security, which during the transition period is conceived in terms of wealth and material comfort. Sex, not yet an end in itself, remains functional, but the function is no longer reproduction. One cannot, of course, give dates to this transitional process; it is actually a state of mind. As I have suggested, it has been going on slowly and unnoticed for centuries, although from the viewpoint of literary representation it picked up momentum and gained a great deal of notice during and immediately after World War II. It is a state of mind characterized not so much by a search for new meaning or truth as by the desire to adapt new situations, experiences and awareness to what are believed to be the old, established values, with resulting confusion and often a sense of guilt.

Of the Canadian novels which explore this state of mind, the following five are especially significant: Gabrielle Roy's *Bonheur d'occasion*—a book, incidentally, which suffered much in translation, as any

Montrealer will immediately realize when startled by a
famous old district being referred to in the translation as
"the Saint Charles Point"—then W.O. Mitchell's *Who
Has Seen the Wind*, Hugh MacLennan's *The Watch that
Ends the Night*, Gérard Bessette's *La Bagarre* and John
Marlyn's *Under the Ribs of Death*.

Gabrielle Roy's *Bonheur d'occasion* mainly concerns
a family living in a Montreal slum. Azarius Lacasse, the
father, works on and off, and the family never has
sufficient for its needs. Always behind in rent, they
must shift from one brokendown flat to another every
spring. Rose-Anna, the mother, follows the old farm
practice of a baby every year or so, pitifully attempting
to adapt her situation to the old order of values,
satisfied that she has, as she puts it, "enduré son
purgatoire sur terre." Like the child Brian in Mitchell's
Who Has Seen the Wind, she struggles to achieve a concept of God, and although she does not arrive at anything
quite so anthropomorphic as "R.W. God, B.V. D.," she is
equally unorthodox when she says, "Maybe he forgets
sometimes. He's bothered with an awful lot of
headaches." And we are told that "the only crack in her
faith came from this candid supposition that God,
distracted, tired, harassed like herself, had come to the
point where he couldn't pay much attention to human
needs."[4] Alex Hunter in Marlyn's *Under the Ribs of
Death* echoes Rose-Anna when he muses to himself:
"Was there a presence interested enough? Perhaps this
being, if it did exist, acted upon motives as inexplicable
and capricious as his own." (p. 211) But the child Brian
probably expresses what is in the minds of all of
these characters when in reply to his grandmother's
statement, "The why—that's another thing. That's for the
Lord," he says, "God isn't very considerate—is He,
Gramma?" (p. 170)

In these novels, then, and in MacLennan's *The Watch
that Ends the Night* and Bessette's *La Bagarre*, the notion

of God as dispenser of the divine order is disappearing, but there is a lingering doubt, with the result that many of the characters are confused, confused about themselves, about their duty and about society. The protagonist of *La Bagarre*, Lebeuf, who is working as a tramway sweeper to pay his way through university, does not know what to do when another of the sweepers begs him to help his daughter. The girl, Gisèle, is exceptionally pretty and intelligent, and the father is afraid that the local priest will parley her into becoming a nun. He is careful to add, "Les curés, moué, j'ai rien contre, r'marque ben." (p. 51) Lebeuf finally suggests that the girl take a job and follow courses part-time at Sir George Williams University, for the idea of part-time studies has been only recently introduced to French-Canadian institutions. But the suggestion of George Williams worries Gisèle's father. "L'instruction, j'sus pour cent pour cent," he replies."Seulement, l'école anglaise, c'est une autre paire de manches, tu comprends..."

In each of the five novels, two or more generations are presented, and there is always a contrast of values between the generations. Gisèle, for example, has ideas of her own, which do not include fitting into any preconceived pattern of divine order. She has found out that men notice her. Florentine, Rose-Anna's daughter in *Bonheur d'occasion*, has gone even further—she has found the possibility of exploiting sexual desire. Sally, in *The Watch that Ends the Night*, because of reasonably affluent circumstances is not quite a budding Sister Carrie like Gisèle and Florentine, but, as she tells her stepfather George, she does not intend to make the mistakes his generation made. She agrees with her boyfriend Allan that they ought to go for a weekend up north. "How is he going to know if he really wants to marry me," she asks George, "unless he's found out first if I'm any good?" (p. 64) All these girls are determined to find emotional security and material comfort whatever way they can; each one of them is a remarkable contrast to Maria Chapdelaine.

The young men in these novels are even more determined than the girls. There is Lebeuf in *La Bagarre* but the characters of Jean Lévesque in *Bonheur d'occasion* and Alex Hunter in *Under the Ribs of Death* are clearer examples. Both are blood brothers of Joe Lampton in John Braine's *Room at the Top*, born on the wrong side of the tracks, tough, cunning, ruthless when necessary, and ready to use almost any means to get to the other side of the tracks. Jean Lévesque can force himself to abandon Florentine when it becomes apparent that she will only be in his way. Alex Hunter can abandon his family, his ethnic group, his very name and identity. But each of these young men must pay the price of recurring doubts, guilt feelings and isolation.

Along with most of the other characters, they must suffer. They must suffer because a sense of security comes essentially from within, from the kind of conviction of a Samuel Chapdelaine or John Elliot. They replace the land by material goods, and, not yet able to divorce their minds from the old system, they presuppose an order which is not there. And worse, whose non-existence is repeatedly demonstrated. Capricious as it is, the land cannot disappear as can worldly wealth during an economic depression, and spring is always sure to follow a winter. With regard to the characters in MacLennan's *The Watch that Ends the Night*, they embrace the supposed new order of socialism, panacea of the sick society, only to be largely disillusioned in the end.

In the five novels, there are many more characters than those already mentioned, a great variety in fact, for each of the authors is especially skilful at delineating character. Common to all of these books, however, is a character who acts as a background against which the anxieties of the other characters can be more readily grasped. In *Who Has Seen the Wind*, it is the Ben, and the young Ben also. In *Bonheur d'occasion*, it is Alphonse, who has been raised in a shack on the city dump. In *La Bagarre*, it is Margeurite, Lebeuf's mistress, although not enough is said about her to make her as obvious as the others. In *Under the Ribs of Death*, it is Uncle Janos, and in *The Watch that Ends the Night*, it is the major character Jerome. What all these characters have in common is that they exist in amoral worlds of their own, essentially unimpressed by the conventions of the society around them. They can avoid the ordinary problems of living and adjusting, because they instinctively obey some internal animal force. When these people do have trouble, it is because of a conflict between themselves and the immediate society. The Ben must find a new hiding place for his still, and he joins the church so that he can become its janitor and keep his still in the church basement. Alphonse and his father must leave their shack in the dump when the shanty town is burned to the ground by city officials. Jerome, by far the most complex of the group, automatically does what George and other men cannot do: he fulfils the life of a woman with a weak heart by impregnating her and risking her death. And it works, because it is a private affair and the woman has full confidence in him. But in the army and the medical profession he continually runs into difficulties with duty and authority.

The type of conflict which people such as Jerome and the Ben experience, however, is seldom within themselves, as is the case with so many of the other characters. They may be philosophers of a sort, but they are not the creators of philosophical systems, because they function mainly from impulse. They learn by experience, as did Jerome in the war, or as the Ben when he decided to free his caged owl after spending time in jail. There is something of the wild creature in all of them, and they are associated with a wild or natural environment in some way: the lumber camp, the city dump and the prairie for Jerome, Alphonse and the Ben; the dream of Margeurite to set up a little motel in the country with Lebeuf; the stories of Uncle Janos's adventures as a sea captain. All these characters seem to exude an aura of self-reliance and independence which becomes a source of fascination for others. Divorced from external order and concepts of order, they remain basically unaffected by the breakup of the old order, and they serve to underline the instability and arti- ficiality of a society incapable of coordinating its own realities with its assumed ethical values.

The third major thematic idea of the French- Canadian and English-Canadian novel is "The Search for Vital Truth". This idea has revealed itself especially in novels of the last five or ten years, in particular Douglas Le Pan's *The Deserter*, Hubert Aquin's *Prochain Episode*, Jacques Godbout's *Le Couteau sur la table*, and Leonard Cohen's *Beautiful Losers*. The search for meaning, of course, can be found in a large number of books, but the kind of search I have in mind here is in a special category—it begins at the zero point. All values have been discarded or cannot be genuinely accepted, and the protagonist attempts from his experience of life to formulate an approach to reality which can supply him with a *raison d'être*. Whereas with Brian in *Who Has Seen the Wind*, or George in *The Watch that Ends the Night*, or Alex Hunter, or Lebeuf there is primarily a struggle of adaptation, in the works of Le Pan, Aquin, Cohen and Godbout it is a matter of creation, creation from the raw materials of personal experience.

In each of these novels the protagonist has withdrawn from his family and conventional society. Rusty in *The Deserter*, the only central character of the four books who is given a name at all, and the protagonist of *Le*

Couteau both leave the army; the central figure in *Beautiful Losers* is living in a treehouse, and the hero of *Prochain Episode* is in jail for terrorist activities. In Aquin's novel the story shifts between the prisoner's introspection and the narration of events leading up to his arrest.

All four novels dwell upon the influence of what can be called peak moments—brief periods when the character achieves a harmonic of mental, spiritual and physical satisfaction, an experience of beauty which is equated with truth. These periods seem almost independent of space and time, and the descriptions of them in each book involve a type of imagery suggestive of a return to the pristine condition. For the central characters the peak moment is also associated with sexual experience and a particular woman. Edith in *Beautiful Losers*, K in *Prochain Episode*, Althea in *The Deserter* and Patricia in *Le Couteau* are remarkably similar. Each is physically beautiful; in fact, each of these creatures is simply the embodiment of physical female beauty, special attention being paid by all four authors to the magnificence of the thighs. It is as if these girls had been created by A.J.M. Smith's sorcerer in Lachine, for they can permit an experience removed from thought, morality, lust or inhibition of any kind. But they cannot voluntarily permit a repetition of this superb experience. As Cohen writes: "it was just a shape of Edith: then it was just a humanoid shape; then it was just a shape—and for a blessed second truly I was not alone, I was part of a family. That was the first time we made love. It never happened again. Is that what you will cause me to feel, Catherine Tekakwitha? But aren't you dead? How do I get close to a dead saint? The pursuit seems like such nonsense." (p. 96)

Catherine Tekakwitha, by the way, is the venerated Iroquois virgin, converted by the Jesuits, who died in 1680 from self-inflicted mortification of the flesh.

Cohen's *Beautiful Losers*, its meaning perhaps somewhat obscured by an overload of sordid detail which has caused the book to be gravely misjudged by a number of reviewers, uses this extreme religious fanatic as a symbol of absolute conviction. The conviction is morbid and perverted, but it still represents a vivid antithesis to current nothingness, a condition of mind otherwise only relieved by the peak moment and the kind of conviction associated with Québec Separatism, the positive psychological value of which is underlined by Cohen, Godbout, and Aquin. Cohen goes further than Le Pan, Aquin, perhaps even Godbout, in creating an impression of the spiritual bankruptcy of the age. His pseudo-character F. is symbolic of the physical, sensual aspects of man, and the surface homosexual relationship between the protagonist and F. represents modern man's frantic search for sensual experience, his worship of the body beautiful, the sex kitten, the pop society's conscious or unconscious fascination with the forbidden, the novel or the perverted. F.'s legacy of soap, cosmetics and firecrackers is symbolic of various sensations, those connected with World War II and family life being appropriately denied the protagonist.

Godbout also creates a strong atmosphere of spiritual bankruptcy, but dwells more upon social, political aspects than upon sex and sensation. His method, however, is very similar to Cohen's. Both authors employ what Cohen describes as "the newsreel escaped into the feature," a mixture of fact and fiction, abandoning traditional narrative and plot for a numbered series of small sections, each concerned with an aspect of the protagonist's consciousness. Godbout incorporates liberal amounts of English into his text, and Cohen does the same with French. Heroines in both books are crushed to death, and at the end both protagonists enter a self-effacing identification fantasy. Cohen's device of the protagonist's impossible desire for union with the Iroquois virgin, Catherine Tekakwitha, provides a fascinating dramatization of the search theme.

There is little satire in any of the four novels, for each of the central characters is more concerned with the annihilation of his own identity and the search for a vital truth to justify his existence than with what may be wrong or false in the society around him. The emptiness of the society is communicated, but not satirized. Rusty discovers the underworld of misfits and criminals created in the aftermath of World War II. Many of the people he meets are like the Ben, as is the Mexican Pedro in *Le Couteau*; they are able to function on the impulse level and thereby achieve an enviable primitive happiness. "Only be careful not to think, or look closely, or ask questions, or play the intellectual," the narrator in *Le Couteau* says of Pedro.[5] In *Beautiful Losers*, F. writes to the protagonist: "You plague me like the moon. I knew you were bound by old laws of suffering and obscurity." (p. 159) And Le Pan writes of Rusty: "After his vigil with Steve it cheered him to think of them feasting and moving on, knowing the world was desperate but not caring, baiting it, challenging it with its own heat, guardians and wastrels of its most essential carnal warmth. They would create festivals in the cold, he was sure, wherever they were. He was glad they existed, although he was shut out of their perfection too." (p. 260) A subtle change in attitude has thus taken place since the novels treating the second major theme: people like the Ben are no longer the oddballs and outcasts, but are now the possessors of a kind of perfection. And the problem for Rusty and for the three other main characters is that they cannot submerge their intellects. They are the victims of their own honesty, intelligence and awareness, stranded without an engagable point of reference. Nor can they be sustained by a projection or continuum of peak

20

moments; they cannot cross the river of meaning by hopping from the stone of one sensual experience to another.

Douglas Le Pan differs from the other three authors in that he concludes *The Deserter* on a mildly positive note. Rusty eventually accepts that life is a shared experience, demanding sacrifice and only occasionally providing a glimpse of self-fulfilment, a complexity of animal, emotional and intellectual aspects, devoid of any superimposed order, yet still permitting the individual through involvement to breed a personal order and meaning around himself. He is a long way from the rationale of Samuel Chapdelaine and John Elliot, for in determining the significance of a human life the emphasis is now on the man rather than an inherited divine order, but there are the common elements of shared experience and sacrifice, and Rusty is finally able to face the world. The protagonist of *Beautiful Losers* comes to a realization of his state, but without Rusty's impetus to commit himself: "O Father, Nameless and Free of Description," he says, "lead me from the Desert of the Possible. Too long I have dealt with Events. Too long I labored to become an Angel. I chased Miracles with a bag of Power to salt their wild Tails. I tried to dominate Insanity so I could steal its Information. I tried to program the Computers with Insanity. I tried to create Grace to prove that Grace existed . . . We could not see the Evidence so we stretched our Memories . . . we did not train ourselves to Receive because we believed there wasn't Anything to Receive and we could not endure with this Belief." (p. 178-9) *Le Couteau* and *Prochain Episode*, on the other hand, both end with a deep sense of frustration, and it would appear that each of the four authors in his own way is close to social and psychological reality.

One thing, however, is clear: considering the particular social climate in which Godbout and Aquin wrote their books, a climate which will be discussed at length in another essay in this volume, and deferring for a moment the universal thematic implications, these two authors are undoubtedly close to Québec reality. In both books the internal frustration of the protagonists is overtly correlated with recent events in French-Canadian society. Godbout actually incorporates into his text, along with statistics on the American nuclear arsenal and various other tragic world developments, a newspaper report of the F.L.Q. bombing which killed an elderly watchman, William O'Neil. Aquin's *Prochain Episode* has an obvious allegorical level of interpretation: the protagonist is French-Canadian youth seeking self-fulfilment, which is equated with independence for French Canada. H. de Heutz, in his various guises, is the power structure associated with English Canada and the federal government. The girl K, object of the protagonist's adoration, is *la patrie*, Québec. The love affair, then, becomes a highly emotional patriotism, and there is the strong implication at the end of the book that K, Québec, has betrayed this patriotic sentiment. The reader is made aware of the possibility that H. de Heutz has some kind of deal with K, for the protagonist overhears a telephone conversation between him and a girl staying at *l'hôtel d'Angleterre.* When the protagonist goes to this hotel for his prearranged rendezvous with K, she has already left.

To pursue this train of thought a little further, it seems to me that the level of interpretation of *Le Couteau* and *Prochain Episode* which has to do with the current situation in Québec is highly revealing, perhaps more revealing than a royal commission report could ever be, because a creative writer is free to use artistic intuition and imagination as well as analysis. Both Godbout and Aquin, and Leonard Cohen to a certain extent also, imply that the present unrest in French Canada has really nothing to do with the question of what French Canadians want. A list of wants can be formulated easily enough, no doubt, but to supply these wants will not solve the problem, which is primarily a community projection of the sense of frustration so effectively dramatized in the work of Godbout and Aquin. Moreover, this sense of frustration is hardly peculiar to Québec, as a number of contemporary novels from several countries reveal, as Godbout himself illustrates with his varied references to the world scene, and as Aquin suggests by his hero's identification with different types of exiles. It has reached, it would seem, a heightened degree in French Canada, but I suspect this is so mainly because in Québec, conveniently, there are all the ingredients for the illusion of a specific cause and a specific solution. What is not illusory, however, is that French Canadians sense and fear that they are being steadily overwhelmed by what they call the Anglo-Saxon mentality or way of life, which is precisely the same thing many English Canadians also fear but refer to as Americanization, which in turn is known to many Americans as the furious dehumanization of the age. In Cohen's *Beautiful Losers*, the idea is arrestingly illustrated in a passage where a Danish vibrating machine comes alive on its own, like a Frankenstein, and succeeds in bringing sexual satisfaction to Edith. Aldous Huxley, an international figure, projected the idea to an ultimate end and called it the Brave New World.

But to get back to the common themes of French-Canadian and English-Canadian literature, it is clear that Douglas Le Pan, Hubert Aquin, Leonard Cohen and Jacques Godbout are all concerned with the same basic problem. Their approaches to the problem, of course, differ. In fact, it is hard to imagine four worlds so completely different as those of the four books in question—Godbout's prairie motels and mobile set, Aquin's Alpine roads and James Bond intrigue, Cohen's Indian legends and sensual fantasies, Le Pan's London dockyards and leftovers of a war. Yet despite these differences, all four novels explore the same emptiness, the same inspiration, the same frustration, and the same major thematic idea of man's quest for vital truth.

It can be safely said, therefore, that French-Canadian and English-Canadian novels of the twentieth century have traced a single basic line of ideological development, creating a whole spectrum of common images, attitudes and ideas. They have done so for the most part independently, each in its own solitude, but obviously we have twin solitudes. In effect, recalling Marius Bewley's statement that writers define nationality, it becomes evident that French Canadians and English Canadians are much more alike than many spokesmen have ever dared to suspect. Aside from language, it is quite probable that there are at the moment no fundamental cultural differences between the two major ethnic groups of Canada. Cohen's *Beautiful Losers* could almost be a sequel to Godbout's *Le Couteau sur la table*. We have evolved according to the same prescription. We have outgrown what differences we may once have had.

It should be pointed out, however, that there are certainly well-established myths to endorse the supposition of two distinctly different cultures, and that these myths have been perpetuated by writers in both languages. Not counting Hugh MacLennan and Canon Lionel Groulx, there are few twentieth-century French-Canadian or English-Canadian writers who have ventured to offer more than a gesture of insight into the other ethnic group. French-Canadian characters can indeed be found in English-Canadian novels—there is Blacky Valois in Allister's *A Handful of Rice*, Gagnon in Callaghan's *The Loved and the Lost* and one of the prostitutes in his *Such is My Beloved*, René de Sevigny in Graham's *Earth and High Heaven*, Frenchy Turgeon in Garner's *Storm Below* and a whole family in his *Silence on the Shore*, and a multitude of others; but these characters are generally either stereotyped or completely out of context. The same situation obtains with the French-Canadian novel. Even Patricia in *Le Couteau* is the familiar stereotype of the wealthy English person from the west side of the Montreal mountain, with a hint of the Hemingway "rich bitch" for colour. Patricia is not in fact of English origin at all, being half-Jewish and half-Irish according to the author; but then even for French-Canadian intellectuals the word *anglais* has always been a very catholic term.

I mentioned Hugh MacLennan and Canon Groulx as exceptions. Groulx, however, is not really an exception to the general rule of mutual ignorance. His *L'Appel de la race*, a novel written in 1922, does indeed consider English Canada, but upon a basis of racist theories which would hardly be taken seriously except in places like South Africa and Alabama. Hugh MacLennan's *Two Solitudes*, on the other hand, is a unique and impressive accomplishment. It has become, almost overnight seemingly, an historical novel. The author set out to dramatize certain basic concepts which conditioned French-Canadian society, and he succeeded in doing so. Some readers in French Canada have been dismayed by the ending of the book and its implication that Paul will be assimilated into the English group. But what in fact happens is that part way through the book MacLennan shifts from dramatization of group concepts to characterization of individuals, so that the dénouement should not be regarded as a prophecy about the future of French Canada. One English-speaking novelist, incidentally, did in fact predict that French-Canadians would be assimilated, and with great rapidity. That novelist was Frances Brooke, and her prophecy was made in the year 1769.

With Hugh MacLennan's *Two Solitudes* as a partial exception, the two literary traditions of Canada have remained essentially isolated. In a recent issue of *la*

revue Liberté, (No. 42) Naïm Kattan suggested that so
far as the English-language tradition is concerned, the
individual writers are even isolated from one another.
But I don't think that Mr. Kattan is entirely correct. Even
though geographically separated, the major writers of
English Canada are undoubtedly aware of each other's
work, possibly as much so as French-Canadian writers
living in the same apartment block in Montreal. Mr.
Kattan's real point, however, was that compared to
English-Canadian novelists, the novelists of French
Canada are a far more homogeneous group, which is
true. They are also, I might add, so productive that if an
outside observer were asked to indicate which of the
two language groups in Canada is in greater danger of
disappearing culturally, he would very probably pick the
English Canadian.

At the moment, for instance, an intriguing linguistic
experiment is taking place. Jacques Renaud in *Le Cassé*,
Claude Jasmin, Gérald Godin, and Laurent Girouard in
parts of *La Ville inhumaine* have elected to use *joual*,
the Québec dialect, as a literary language. The critics for
the most part are either uncertain about the significance
of this phenomenon, or they condemn it outright as a
kind of submission to corruption. *Joual* certainly is a
conglomeration of corruptions, contractions, archaisms,
mispronunciations, loan words and innovations—
which, of course, is precisely what French was
before the Isle de France standard and the formidable
Académie française, or what English was and regional,
spoken English still is. Any notion of legitimacy in
language must perforce be a figment of the purist's
imagination. But be that as it may, the recent experiments with *joual* could have far-reaching effect. One has
only to recall the influence of Mark Twain on American
literature or the cultural explosion in Norway with the
creation of a distinctive Norwegian language based upon
rural dialects. Some French-Canadian critics may well be

lamenting the very initiative which will lead to a distinguishing idiom.

To return once more to the comparative novel, one last question remains to be considered, the question of national identity with which we began. It has been shown that in the course of twentieth-century evolution, principal novels in French and English Canada have embraced the same spectrum of attitudes and ideas, albeit separately. What has this phenomenon to do with the definition of national identity? Has our literature produced one, or two, or no definitions?

In the first place, if the notable parallels in French-Canadian and English-Canadian literature have any significance at all, then it must be because there does exist a single, common national mystique, a common set of conditioning forces, the mysterious apparatus of a single sense of identity. But, nevertheless, I think that our literature has not yet succeeded in providing more than an embryonic definition of nationality. The reasons for this lack of success up to now are probably myriad. We have moved through stages of masochistic resignation and dependence, as illustrated in the works of Hémon, Grove and Ringuet, of confusion and struggle of adaptation, as seen in novels by Roy, MacLennan, Mitchell, Bessette and Marlyn, and we are at the moment groping simultaneously with the very essence of truth. We have not had an intellectual climate of positive myth and idealism to work within, as the Americans have had for instance. We have always known that this country is not the "garden of the world", and any notions of "manifest destiny" the French-Canadian explorers possessed, long ago went down the drain. There has been too much of the Catherine Tekakwitha in us for our own good. We, French Canadians and English Canadians, have perversely insisted upon isolation and upon stereotyped images of each other, and like the characters in Le Pan,

Cohen, Aquin and Godbout, or even in MacLennan's *Barometer Rising*, we know what we are not, but we are either unwilling or still incapable of articulating what we are. Yet, as this essay has attempted to demonstrate, a process of involuntary consolidation of literary efforts has begun to take effect, and an emerging national mystique is somehow dictating the themes of Canadian creative writing. As Dave Godfrey implies in his subtle allegory "The Hard-Headed Collector," the diverse cultural traditions transplanted to Canada have all had their conditioning effect, but none has dominated or even flourished. And we find ourselves with withered roots instead of the orchard which might have been. Yet somehow the living remnants may join together to form a uniquely Canadian myth, at once ancient and contemporary.

This process could be strengthened by a greater mutual knowledge on the part of both major groups of Canadians and an increase in comparative studies. More and better translations would be useful. But even of greater benefit for French-Canadian novels, so many of which contain excellent colloquial dialogue, would be a series of annotated editions, providing in appendices (or in footnotes as in the recent Toronto edition of Pierre Gravel's *A Perte de temps*) translations of difficult expressions, somewhat as the standard editions of Chaucer do. In any event, I think that we are now at a stage of genuine mutual interest, which is likely to be sustained. It seems also likely that as mutual knowledge of French-Canadian and English-Canadian literature increases, as we become more aware of the significant parallels between the two, both bodies of literature will increase in scope and power, and we shall at the same time move toward a positive sense and adequate definition of Canadian identity.

The Body-Odour of Race

The problem of race and ethnic relations has never been a major concern of Canadian literature. By contrast, the great American classics—*Moby Dick*, the Leather-stocking tales, *Huckleberry Finn*—have all focused upon the communion between persons of different races, and this theme has persisted in the works of Faulkner, Porter, Baldwin, Ellison and many others. These writers, it would seem, either concluded or sensed that the realization of the American Dream, indeed the survival of the American nation, would depend upon the ability of people of different ethnic origins to learn to live with each other in a mutually satisfactory manner. And to the outside observer of the United States, it is becoming increasingly clear that this thesis is all too true. As a matter of fact, we can go a step further than the survival of the United States—it is now clear that the survival of man will be ultimately determined by the capacity of the various peoples of the world to live together in reasonable harmony.

For Canadians, looking at the problems south of the border has long been a comfortable spectator sport. It is right that American authors should be preoccupied with race and ethnic relations—after all, the Americans brought most of their miseries upon themselves, and the Negro situation in the United States, because of hardcore ignorance and prejudice, has progressed no more than from a frightening atrocity into a frightening mess. In Canada, on the other hand, all has gone relatively well. There are not enough Negroes to create a real disturbance, and the most prominent are generally great athletes or football stars who seem satisfied to function as idols in a nation of the under-exercised. Outside of the occasional claim on real estate in downtown Brantford, Ontario, or the contention that old treaties entitle them to all the amenities of modern medicine, or slight misunderstandings about what constitutes a murder, Canadian Indians and Eskimos have come up with very little that the R.C.M.P. could not handle. The tourist trade, profitable sale of little birchbark canoes, structural steel construction jobs for the more energetic, and the complete annihilation of the Beothuks of Newfoundland before they could become a problem, have all helped to preserve the national peace of mind. And so far as the Jews are concerned, they have always seemed to fit quite smoothly into the Canadian scene, if not entirely so into the stock exchanges and the school commissions. Indeed, Jewish writers have made such a disproportionate contribution to what is significant in Canadian Letters that without them the field would be a Barebones parliament, complete with generous share of Roundheads.

There has been, nevertheless, and there continues to be a great deal of friction in Canada between what are sometimes referred to as the two "founding races"— English-speaking Canadians and French Canadians. Of

course, in the strictest anthropological sense the term
"race" should not be used to distinguish either of the
two major ethnic groups of Canada from the other. So
far as I can determine, there is no true racial divergence
between French and English Canadians. *Les Canadiens*,
having come largely from Normandy, Brittany and
Picardy, are the result of a mixture of many strains,
including the Celts, Germanic tribes such as the Franks,
Jutes and Frisians as well as the Norsemen or Normans,
not to mention a number of exiled Highland Scots and
wandering Irishmen. English-speaking Canadians, strange
as it may appear to some, are more or less a blend of
exactly the same elements, with a good measure of
Norman-French blood thrown in besides. The notion of
a uniform *mentalité anglo-saxonne*, despite the exclama-
tions in Daniel Johnson's book *Egalité ou Indépendance*, cannot be taken seriously by anyone who has
actually lived in Britain, Canada and the United States.
Like that other catch-all, "the Latin temperment," it is
a term far easier to use than to justify, and I strongly
suspect that both of these expressions, handy as they
may be to resolve the irresolute, are completely
meaningless.

The fact, nevertheless, that there are no true racial
differences between English- and French-speaking
Canadians has not prevented the emergence, reflected in
Canadian literature, of the ugly phenomenon known as
racism. A set of attitudes which has single-handedly
filled the chamber of twentieth-century horrors, racism
is defined in the Standard College Dictionary as "an
excessive and irrational belief in or advocacy of the
superiority of a given group, people, or nation, usually
one's own, on the basis of racial differences having no
scientific validity." Racism, then, does not require that
there be any real differences of race; it simply requires
an irrational belief in the superiority of a given group on
the grounds of supposed differences. In Canada, com-

pared to the United States and South Africa, racist
attitudes have often been well-disguised, of a subtle and
covert nature, aroused in many instances by individuals
and small groups to exploit a particular situation.

In his poem "Political Meeting," the Montreal poet
A.M. Klein put his finger on it brilliantly. The poem
concerns a rally addressed by Camillien Houde, the
former Mayor of Montreal, in the wake of the con-
scription crisis in 1942. I can recall as a small boy
witnessing such rallies, and I have always marvelled at
the power and detailed accuracy of Klein's description
—the absence of the religious brothers, signifying the
Church's unsure position, the singing of "Alouette," the
joual, the clever turn of phrase, the hypnotic force of a
skilled orator. But here is the poem:

On the school platform, draping the folding seats,
they wait the chairman's praise and glass of water.
Upon the wall the agonized Y initials their faith.

Here all are laic; the skirted brothers have gone.
Still, their equivocal absence is felt, like a breeze
that gives curtains the sounds of surplices.

The hall is yellow with light, and jocular;
suddenly some one lets loose upon the air
the ritual bird which the crowd in snares of singing

catches and plucks, throat, wings, and little limbs.
Fall the feathers of sound, like *alouette's*.
The chairman, now, is charming, full of asides and wit,

building his orators, and chipping off
the heckling gargoyles popping in the hall.
(Outside, in the dark, the street is body-tall,

flowered with faces intent on the scarecrow thing
that shouts to thousands the echoing
of their own wishes.) The Orator has risen!

Worshipped and loved, their favorite visitor,
a country uncle with sunflower seeds in his pockets,
full of wonderful moods, tricks, imitative talk,

he is their idol: like themselves, not handsome,
not snobbish, not of the *Grand Allée! Un homme!*
Intimate, informal, he makes bear's compliments

to the ladies; is gallant; and grins;
goes for the balloon, his opposition, with pins;
jokes also on himself, speaks of himself

in the third person, slings slang, and winks with
                                                    folklore;
and knows now that he has them, kith and kin.
Calmly, therefore, he begins to speak of war,

praises the virtue of being *Canadien*,
of being at peace, of faith, of family,
and suddenly his other voice: *Where are your sons?*

He is tearful, choking tears; but not he
would blame the clever English; in their place
he'd do the same; maybe.

Where *are* your sons?
                    The whole street wears one face,
shadowed and grim; and in the darkness rises
the body-odor of race.

Before considering the observations made by
Canadian writers on racism and cultural identity, however, I wish to examine certain racist ideas which can be
found in the personal philosophies of a few Canadian
writers themselves. I have tried to limit the examination
to certain significant authors and to those ideas
which by virtue of being apparently widespread
or especially persistent, continue to have reper-
cussions in our own day. It is necessary, also, to try
to distinguish between the conviction of superiority

which characterizes racism and simple cases of exaggerated pride in the presumed merits of one's ethnic group.

Among minor writers of English Canada, for instance, there have been many who were carried away by exaggerated pride. One need only glance through Edward Hartley Dewart's *Selections from Canadian Poets* to find choice examples. Here is Charles Sangster, a poet of considerable talent in more sober moments, beginning his "Song for Canada":

> Sons of the race whose sires
> Aroused the martial flame,
> That filled with smiles
> The triune Isles,
> Through all their heights of fame!
>
> With hearts as brave as theirs,
> With hopes as strong and high,
> We'll ne'er disgrace
> The honored race
> Whose deeds can never die. (p. 106)

More apropos, perhaps, in this time of bilingual cheques and bonused government clerks, are lines such as the following from Pamela Vining's "Canada":

> Forests, whose echoes never had been stirred
> By the sweet music of an English word,
> Where only rang the red-browed hunter's yell,
> And the wolf's howl through the dark sunless dell.
> (p. 102)

And one could go on and on. But verses such as these merely indicate an overflow of spontaneous patriotism, coloured by a normal enough preference for one's own ethnic culture. There is a profound difference, it seems

to me, between this kind of expression and the attitude
which can be detected in the work of Susanna Moodie,
the English lady who roughed it in the bush—to a
certain extent, that is. For she was seldom reduced so
low as to be without servants and a good liquor supply.

Mrs. Moodie was manifestly convinced of the
superiority of the particular class of English gentlefolk
to which she belonged, and she makes the idea clear in
passages such as the following in her book *Roughing It
in the Bush:*

> The hand that has long held the sword, and been
> accustomed to receive implicit obedience from those
> under its control, is seldom adapted to wield the spade
> and guide the plough, or try its strength against the
> stubborn trees of the forest. Nor will such persons
> submit cheerfully to the saucy familiarity of servants,
> who, republicans in spirit, think themselves as good as
> their employers. (pp. xviii-xix)

Moodie makes the same point many times, always
carefully differentiating between "superiors" and
"inferiors". She speaks of the "vicious, uneducated
barbarians, who form the surplus of over-populated
European countries." At one point she observes: "The
semi-barbarous Yankee squatters, who had 'left their
country for their country's good,' and by whom we
were surrounded in our first settlement, detested us..."
And to this last remark of Susanna Moodie's, one is
tempted to reply "No Wonder." In many respects her
classification of people is reminiscent of Samuel
Richardson in *Sir Charles Grandison*, where he divided
his characters into three categories: men, women and
Italians. Only for Moodie the classes would be English
gentlemen, English ladies and barbarians.

Of course, her standards for herself were exceedingly
high. Here she is admitting to an "unpardonable
weakness":

In spite of my boasted fortitude—and I think my
powers of endurance have been tried to the utmost
since my sojourn in this country—the rigour of the
climate subdued my proud, independent English spirit,
and I actually shamed my womanhood, and cried with
the cold. Yes, I ought to blush at confessing such
unpardonable weakness; but I was foolish and in-
experienced, and unaccustomed to the yoke. (p. 159)

After having read the works of Susanna Moodie, one
is left with the undeniable impression that everybody—
Irish, French-Canadian, Scottish, Indian, lowborn
English and especially American—who is not of her
particular caste has been hopelessly predestined to
insignificance, *ipso facto*. Moreover, her attitude, which
appears to be essentially unconscious and without
malicious intent, led her to remarkable conclusions on
occasion. Speaking of the cholera doctor Stephen Ayres,
for instance, she comments: "A friend of mine, in this
town, has an original portrait of this notable empiric—
this man sent from heaven. The face is rather handsome,
but has a keen, designing expression, and is evidently
that of an American from its complexion and features."
(p. 54)

Now it may appear to some that I have been
looking at the writings of Susanna Moodie with a
magnifying glass, considering that she did no more than
echo the accepted English spirit of her time, but
certainly through a magnifying glass is the way Mrs.
Moodie consistently looked at herself. I do not deny the
merits of her literary achievement—her keen eye for
appropriate detail, her ear for dialect, her capacity to
capture scenes and moods. Nevertheless, throughout her
work, as throughout the works of Ralph Connor, to
name one other obvious example, there is always the
disconcerting body-odour of race, the undertone of
racism. Not the screeching, messianic racism of a

Houston Stewart Chamberlain, the man who talked with demons and who sowed the field which Adolf Hitler was to harvest, but something perhaps almost as malignant in the long run, because it is in the form of a deeply ingrained pattern of thought, a conviction which may even be unconsciously held. Furthermore, it is the very conviction which in various guises has haunted and continues to haunt a nation which, if it is going to survive, must perforce develop a *modus vivendi* for people of different ethnic origins.

Moodie herself, it should be pointed out, merely chanted a common tendency of many nations, a tendency which was perhaps an inevitable adjunct to strong cultural identification, a tendency which in most circumstances was probably not of great harm or consequence. What is important to us here is that the Moodie attitude has not died a natural death, but continues to infect the thinking of many English Canadians, and that in the particular circumstances of modern Canada it could be of vital consequence.

It is the kind of attitude, whether conscious or unconscious, which has often thrown up a formidable psychological barrier to satisfactory and harmonious relations between Canada's two major ethnic groups. One becomes aware of it in letters to the editor, in statements by university professors, in the interpretations of Canadian history by certain prominent historians, in pronouncements of the Canadian Legion, in parliamentary speeches, in the Protestant school boards of the Province of Québec which objected to the suggestion of the Parent Commission that they integrate with the French Catholic system. For, as members of school boards are quick to explain, it is well-known that the English Protestant system has always been superior to its French-Canadian counterpart, and for obvious reasons.

A number of English-Canadian writers, especially in

recent years, have been conscious of the lingering miasma of racism in Canada. They have dramatized and satirized it, moving further and further away from the spirit typified by Susanna Moodie. As Canadian poets have turned from landscapes to social and psychological realities, they have become increasingly sensitive to the false values in established Canadian patterns of thought and have reflected this sensitivity in their poems. Among the more obvious examples are Earle Birney's "Anglosaxon Street", Frank Scott's "The Canadian Social Register", and Ralph Gustafson's "Psalm 23". In several poems by Irving Layton, A.J.M. Smith or Alfred Purdy, one finds less explicit but equally effective reaction to the Moodie attitude. In the area of prose writing, Sara Jeannette Duncan's *The Imperialist* reveals a tone in striking contrast to that found in Susanna Moodie's work. Mitchell's *Who Has Seen the Wind*, Ross's *As For Me and My House*, Graham's *Earth and High Heaven*, and especially Hugh MacLennan's *Barometer Rising* and *Two Solitudes* may be added to the list.

It is of interest to note, incidentally, that whenever there is a confrontation of races or ethnic groups coupled with racist ideas, a variety of myths inevitably spring up. In the United States, there is the well-known myth of the extraordinary virility of the Negro, which most probably arose from the fear that the Negro constituted a threat to the supposed purity of the white race. Stressing in its earliest form the idea that the Negro male was possessed of violent, uncontrollable animal passions, it presumably acted as a taboo to protect white women. The cohabiting of white men with Negro women, of course, was always regarded as a special service to genetic improvement.

Now in Canada, one ethnic myth which has developed is that the French-Canadian girl is more highly sexed than her English-speaking compatriot, and this myth, still very much alive, has had a whole complexity of effects. It is difficult to say exactly how such a myth could have taken root. As Gilles Marcotte points out in his *Une Littérature qui se fait*, (p. 15) a series of early French-Canadian novels, seemingly in an attempt to coat the pill of military defeat, presented love affairs between British men and alluring French-Canadian maidens, and in each of these affairs the girl, having reduced her suitor to blubbering incapacity, haughtily refuses to marry him. The best of these novels, Philippe Aubert de Gaspé's *Les anciens Canadiens*, a book rich in fascinating detail about early Canadian life and mores, tells how the handsome Archibald Cameron of Locheill, desperately in love with Blanche d'Haberville since the prewar days when he had lived in Québec as a guest of her family, is forced to take part in the defeat of the French régime and consequently loses his true love.

Perhaps the romance theme in novels such as *Les anciens Canadiens* had something to do with the emergence of the French-Canadian-girl myth. A more probable explanation, however, is racist conviction of the type seen in Susanna Moodie's writing. Since the possibility of ethnic intermixture in colonial Canada almost exclusively involved English men and French-Canadian women, the English women being either here with their husbands or left at home, the myth focused on the threat of the French-Canadian female rather than the male. When, for example, Frances Brooke, in *The History of Emily Montague*, is not ranting about "the mild genius of our religion and laws, and that spirit of industry, enterprize, and commerce, to which we owe all our greatness," she is strongly suggesting through the tone of the letters which make up her novel that French-Canadian girls are abandoned coquettes, more passionate than sensible, with a definite inclination toward seducing the unwary English gentleman. Thus it seems quite plausible that the myth of *la femme fatale canadienne* traces back to the feeling of superiority and female possessiveness of the colonial English ladies.

In addition to the myth just described, there are several others, such as the notion that French Canadians are deficient in business sense, or that Roman Catholicism and the French language are mystically interdependent. These last two are now in a state of decreasing currency and may soon disappear entirely. The sex myth of the French-Canadian girl, however, like the sex myth of the Negro, continues to hold ground because of an intriguing reversal of social perspectives. When these myths emerged, the ascendency of the animal passions was generally held to be the essence of human depravity. But in the last few decades, positions have changed drastically, and now any indication of powerful heterosexual drive, reasonably free from neuroses, perversions and inhibitions, is regarded as a recommendation rather than a condemnation. Consequently, the erstwhile targets of these sex myths have now become the content guardians. The chickens have come home to roost!

Turning to the literature of French Canada, it must be said at the outset that the kind of racism which has found its way into the works of certain French-Canadian writers is more obtrusive than that in English-Canadian books, sometimes entirely devoid of subtlety. This fact is both a good and a bad thing. It is good in that readers have been able to apprehend immediately the position of a particular author and to react accordingly. It is bad in that some have reacted by embracing the racist attitudes extolled. In the case of Lionel Groulx's *L'Appel de la race*, for instance, such distinguished critics as Camille Roy, who was to become Rector of Laval University, Louvigny de Montigny, and René du Roure, Stephen Leacock's old friend, reacted immediately against the thesis presented by Groulx. On the other hand, the influence of Lionel Groulx through his writings in history and literary history as well as the novel in question, has been immense and remains unbelievably strong. Seldom has a man with so many misguided ideas been able to guide so many. Though there *are* some other obvious examples.

L'Appel de la race is the story of a man called Jules de Lantagnac who goes to a classical college, then completes law studies at McGill. He sets up practice in Ottawa and manages to build a clientele of prosperous businessmen. Eventually he marries an English-Canadian girl called Maud Fletcher, after she has changed her religion. They have four children—Wolfred, Nellie, Virginia and William—who, naturally enough, grow up speaking the language of their mother. The boys eventually attend the Jesuit's Loyola College in Montreal, and life for a time is peaceful, prosperous and pleasant for everyone. But then Jules de Lantagnac visits some relatives back in Québec, and while there he hears *l'appel de la race*. He becomes possessed of guilt feelings about having betrayed his ancestry. Upon his return to Ottawa, he begins regular visits to an Oblate priest, Father Fabien, who becomes his personal confessor. He also begins to practise French again, to teach it to his children, and he tries to create in them a sense of their French heritage.

The rest of the book presents a number of startling developments. Jules is elected to Parliament and becomes entangled in the controversy over Bill 17, an unfortunate piece of legislation pertaining to the teaching of French in Ontario schools. Lantagnac is asked to speak against the bill in Parliament, and for reasons that are not made clear his wife Maud decides that if he does make the speech, she will leave him. Lantagnac, accordingly, must choose between his immediate family and his ancestral loyalty. Egged on by Father Fabien, he decides in favour of his ancestors and makes the speech. Then unlike those legions of women who periodically threaten to leave their husbands, Maud sticks to her word, packs her bags and gets out. Nellie and William decide to go with her, while Wolfred and Virginia stay with their father. Virginia finds herself moved to enter a convent, and Wolfred changes his name to André, which is understandable enough under any circumstances.

Now we need not be concerned with the intricacies of the plot of *L'Appel de la race*, nor with the political implications. I, for one, agree with Lionel Groulx that the treatment of French Canadians in school systems outside of Québec has often been a flagrant injustice, brought about mainly by an overdose of the Susanna Moodie creed. What does concern us here, however, is the authorial comment on race contained in Groulx's novel.

Mason Wade, the American historian of French Canada, has observed that "Groulx is a disciple of the historical school of the Count de Gobineau," and "was greatly affected during his studies in Switzerland and France by the anti-democratic ideas of Charles Maurras and Maurice Barrès." (p. 124) Joseph Arthur de Gobineau, of course, is the man who influenced Houston Stewart Chamberlain and whose racist theories prepared the way for Fascist ideology. Gobineau himself, it would appear, never entertained the thought of genocide, but he was greatly instrumental in bringing about that cruel, ironic twist of fate which caused the Jews, whose ancestors invented racism, to become victims of the unspeakable perversions and atrocities which racist theories can so easily promote.

In *L'Appel de la race*, Groulx actually quotes from Barrès and from Dr. Gustave Le Bon's *Lois psychologiques de l'évolution des peuples*, published in 1894. Le Bon, a French doctor and sociologist who died in 1931, published some seventeen volumes over a period

of fifty years. The passage from his work cited by Groulx
is as follows:

> Between two superior races as close to each other as
> the English and Germans of America, crossbreeding
> may be an element of progress. But it always con-
> stitutes an element of degeneration when the races,
> even if superior, are too dissimilar.
> To interbreed two peoples is to change at the same
> time their physical and mental constitutions . . . Thus
> at the beginning the personality remains very irresolute
> and feeble, and it requires a long accumulation of
> hereditary traits to become established. The first
> effect of interbreeding between different races is to
> destroy the racial soul, that is to say the complex of
> ideas and common sentiments which is the strength of
> a people, and without which there can be neither a
> nation nor a homeland . . . It is therefore right that all
> those peoples who have attained a high degree of
> civilization have carefully avoided mixing with
> foreigners.[6]

Lionel Groulx's novel is essentially an application of
these ideas, granting the premise that French and
English Canadians are too dissimilar to be successfully
crossbred, to the situation in Canada. In a conversation
with Lantagnac, Father Fabien says:

> Who knows if our former Canadian aristocracy did not
> owe its decadence to the mixture of bloods which it
> accepted too readily, and too often actually sought
> after. Certainly a psychologist would find it of great
> interest to observe the descendants of that class. Does
> it not seem to you, my friend, that there is a good
> deal of trouble and silly anarchy in the past of these
> old families? How do you explain the delirium, the
> madness with which the offspring of these noblemen

have thrown themselves into dishonour and ruin?[7]

Frantic condemnation of mixed marriages, meaning primarily those between French-speaking and English-speaking Canadians, is splashed throughout the pages of *L'Appel de la race*. Groulx speaks of the "cerebral disorder, the psychological dilution" which results from such ignoble combinations. He is careful to point out, incidentally, that the English are a "superior race" along with the French, but the true texture of his thought comes to the fore in an illuminating manner when he has Lantagnac make the following observations on his four children, to whom he is giving lessons in French:

Lantagnac had only distantly followed the education of his sons and daughters. He knew the basic qualities of their temperaments, but little or nothing about their essential characters. Their success having always been assured by a good measure of intelligence, he had never bothered to think more about them. But now he was discovering in two of his pupils a kind of unhealthy imprecision, a disorder of the thought, an incoherence of the intellect which he did not fully grasp. It was a sort of incapacity to follow a line of reasoning to a conclusion, to concentrate diverse impressions or slightly complex ideas around a central point. It was as if they had in them two souls, two warring spirits which alternately dominated. And strange to say, this mental dualism manifested itself especially in William and Nellie, the two who were predominantly of the well-defined type of the Fletchers. Whereas Wolfred and Virginia almost exclusively resembled the French race, with the fine, bronzed features of the Lantagnacs and the equilibrium of body proportions, the older daughter and younger son, in contrast, with their blond hair and pale complexions, their lanky and somewhat thread-shaped builds, strikingly resembled their mother.[8]

It does not seem to have occurred to Canon Groulx that William and Nellie, as he himself has presented them, were hardly the products of virgin birth, that they had as much redeeming Lantagnac blood in them as Wolfred and Virginia. He takes an almost diabolical delight in describing the younger son, William. At another point in the story he says:

> William remained always the same, with his stubborn and choleric spirit. As he grew older the Saxon traits became stronger in his face and long adolescent's body. The set of his forehead became more rigid, the pout of his lips more arrogant, and one nearly always saw him walking along with his neck arched and his fists half closed, like a rugby player.[9]

With regard to "Saxon traits," by the way, there is some difference of emphasis between Lionel Groulx and Susanna Moodie, as might be expected. Describing her son Donald, Mrs. Moodie says that he had been nicknamed "Cedric the Saxon; and he well suited the name, with his frank, honest disposition, and large, loving, blue eyes." (p. 431)

In the matter of "superior races," then, it is clear that Groulx felt some races to be more superior than others. As a matter of fact, the good canon's most bitter invective is reserved for the Irish Roman Catholics, whom he accuses of serving their Anglo-Saxon masters with a "slave mind." For an historian, incidentally, Lionel Groulx was on many occasions superbly indifferent to history—no "slave mind" his. He seemed to feel so strongly about what he calls "*les affinités profondes*" between French Canadians and Catholicism, that one wonders if he would have included the Pope as a legitimate believer.

But it will serve no good purpose to explore
L'Appel de la race further. The book is a racist,
idiosyncratic morality play, lacking even the merits of a
good description or a clever turn of phrase. Outside of a
small, privately published treatise by Pierre-Paul Rioux
called *L'Espoir du Canada français* and the various
pamphlets written by Adrien Arcand, former leader of
the former Québec Nazi Party, there is nothing else I
know of in Canadian literature that is quite in the same
category. A hint of racism occurs in Félix-Antoine
Savard's *Menaud maître-draveur* but Savard is too
sentimental to be vicious.

So much, then, for the racist ideas in English-
Canadian and French-Canadian literature. If the
expression of these ideas is stronger and more bitter on
the French-Canadian side, the difference in degree is no
doubt explained by the fact that French Canadians have
long felt themselves to be fighting for survival. Susanna
Moodie spoke from a position of security; Lionel
Groulx had his back against the wall. It is therefore
partly understandable that the attitudes of Groulx and
his followers should have gone to extremes, especially
when one considers that they are reactions to similar
attitudes in a presumed opposing camp. Which, of
course, is the ominous aspect of racist tendencies in a
society of mixed ethnic groups—they inevitably produce
a reaction, which inevitably results in a setback for the
cause of tolerance and compatibility. Or to use a phrase
which would perhaps be more meaningful for the
Reverend Canon Groulx, the cause of Christian
brotherhood.

The real purpose of this study, however, is to provide
something more than a display of the dirty linen of
Canadian literature. When a nation is composed of two
major cultural groups, with, as Earle Birney aptly put it,
"parents unmarried and living abroad," and when each
of these groups is susceptible to the very notions most

certain to create misunderstanding and hatred, can a complete breakdown of relations be avoided? Assuming that we want to preserve this single nation (and I think that we have a commitment to do so, a challenge to our resources of humanity and understanding, and a chance to prove a vital principle to the world), is there any way to solve the disease of national schizophrenia? I believe there is, and I think that certain Canadian writers have already provided the diagnosis and treatment.

But before we have a look at these writers, it is necessary to determine exactly what is meant by the terms culture and cultural identity. For clearly the major concern of French Canadians such as Lionel Groulx, and the motivating force behind early Québec separatism, is the avowed desire to preserve an established cultural identity; for English Canadians the big problem of recent years, a problem which has been discussed so often that it is becoming a national neurosis, is to discover whether such an identity actually exists.

The famed comparative ethologist, Konrad Lorenz, in his latest book called *On Aggression*, offers an important insight into the nature of culture. In answer to his own question, "What is culture?" he says:

A system of historically developed social norms and rites which are passed on from generation to generation because emotionally they are felt to be values. What is a value? Obviously, normal and healthy people are able to appreciate something as a high value for which to live and, if necessary, to die, for no other reason than that it was evolved in cultural ritualization and handed down to them by a revered elder. Is, then, a value only defined as the object on which our instinctive urge to preserve and defend traditional social norms has become fixated? Primarily and in the early stages of cultural development this undoubtedly was the case. The obvious advantages of loyal adherence to tradition must have exerted a considerable selection pressure. However, the greatest loyalty and obedience to cultural ritualized norms of behaviour must not be mistaken for responsible morality. Even at their best they are only functionally analogous to behaviour controlled by rational responsibility. (p. 236)

To people like Susanna Moodie, Frances Brooke and Lionel Groulx, this simple, scientific explanation by Konrad Lorenz would be the blackest of heresies against all that is noble, pure and praiseworthy in human experience. Yet, what Lorenz says is unquestionably, indeed startlingly, true. Cultural identification is no more and no less than an emotional involvement, an infatuation if you will, with a particular set of social norms and rites. And in the majority of cases, what are thought of as values are merely the arbitrary "sweet nothings" of an ethnic love affair. It must be pointed out, however, that because cultural identification is not attended by bolts of lightning and a voice from the heavens, it is none the less a necessary condition for the average human being, and particularly for the creative writer. It is as necessary as emotional involvement with other human beings is necessary for the normal person. It provides the framework, the pattern of attitudes and approaches to life which permit the individual to begin functioning meaningfully. But as Konrad Lorenz explains, there is the danger that cultural identification will be confused with rational responsibility, that a person will hold those norms which are sanctioned by his own culture to be absolute moral principles. And because of the high emotional element involved, any attempt to re-establish a proper perspective is like trying to explain reality to a lovesick adolescent.

Taking into account these observations on the signifi-

cance of culture, one must come to the following
conclusion: since the worth of any cultural identity
resides in its usefulness in permitting individuals to
function meaningfully, to adapt to the social and
psychological realities of a particular time and place,
then it is a mistake to think that a culture ought to be
preserved simply because it exists. Fanatic devotion
such as that of Lionel Groulx to any established culture
for its own sake can become childish irresponsibility.
Cultures must evolve with changing patterns of life.
Those aspects of any culture which become obsolete,
which become impediments rather than aids to the
individual in his struggle to achieve a measure of success
and happiness, should *not* be preserved. Let them enter
the realm of nostalgia; let them become art forms along
with Marshall McLuhan's superceded media. For when it
so happens that a particular cultural mystique is
prevented from evolving to fit with reality, the people
who are inadvertently engulfed by that mystique will
suffer undue anxiety and frustration. Lorenz describes
in detail the situation of the Ute Indians in the U.S.A.,
for instance, whose apparatus of cultural identity has
not undergone sufficient adjustment to the modern
American way of life. These Indians suffer more
frequently from neuroses than any other human group,
says Lorenz. But even more fascinating is the fact that
the Ute Indians have a rate of automobile accidents
which "exceeds that of any other car-driving human
group." Now anyone who has had occasion to drive a
car in the province of Québec does not have to
be told that the rate of automobile accidents there is not
far behind that of the Ute Indians. (See: Reports of the
Canadian Highway Safety Council, Ottawa.) And anyone who has read Hubert Aquin's *Prochain Episode* or
Jacques Godbout's *Le Couteau sur la table*, or any of a
dozen other recent French-Canadian novels, will
immediately appreciate how involvement with cultural

50

elements which are maladjusted to reality can produce frustration and despair.

Many French Canadians, of course, have long been aware that the established ethnic culture of French Canada, with its emphasis on unwavering continuity and its isolationist tendencies, has represented an obstacle to progress in a number of fields, including industrialization and education. But one does not erase an emotional involvement in a day or two, as the Lesage government found out when it was removed from office after a programme of much needed modernization. If, however, the culture of French Canada has until recently hindered the group's adaptation to the twentieth century, then the culture of English Canada has been equally effective in hindering that group's adaptation to the fact of French Canada. Distinguished English-Canadian scholars are still descanting upon what was guaranteed or not guaranteed by the British North America Act, as if that mattered a damn when there are social realities to face. And the question remains—what, if anything, can we conclude about all this?

I mentioned earlier that certain works of Canadian literature offer insight into the problem of ethnic groups and cultural identity. In particular, there are Yves Thériault's *Aaron* and Hugh MacLennan's *Two Solitudes*. The first of these novels, *Aaron*, does not in fact deal with relations between French and English Canadians; the story is about a Jewish boy in Montreal. It is of interest to note, moreover, that almost all the recent French-Canadian novels which discuss relations between ethnic groups have involved Jewish characters. These novels include Claire Martin's *Quand j'aurai payé ton visage*, Jacques Godbout's *Le Couteau sur la table*, Robert Goulet's *Charivari*, Claude Jasmin's *Ethel et le terroriste*, and the book which nearly won France's Prix Goncourt, Réjean Ducharme's *L'Avaleé des avalés*. It is evident, however, that in each of these novels the Jewish figure operates as a symbol with which the French Canadian can identify, and that in effect the authors are more or less vicariously exploring the situation of the French-speaking Canadian in North America.

In Thériault's *Aaron*, three possible approaches to culture and cultural identity are outlined. First there is the position of Aaron's grandfather and guardian, Moishe, who sticks to every detail of the Orthodox Jewish culture, ready to endure every inconvenience, refusing to adapt in any way, satisfied to remain poor and despised by many of those in the community around him. Secondly, there is the attitude adopted by Viedna, the beautiful Jewish girl whom young Aaron loved and lost. She decides that the solution to the problem of racial discrimination is simple—one becomes assimilated to another ethnic group. When Aaron meets her again after a long separation and calls her by name, she corrects him. *"Je ne m'appelle plus Viedna. Je m'appelle Cécile,"* she says. Then she goes on to explain:

> You remember I spoke to you about it, Aaron. The only condition of survival is this—stop being Jewish. The Jew can accomplish anything, provided he is no longer Jewish. Consequently . . . we are French, you see? My father is pulling certain strings to obtain French citizenship for us.[10]

The third position is that initially decided upon by Aaron himself. He will continue to think of himself as a Jew, he will not try to be what he is not. At the same time, he does not wish to follow in his grandfather Moishe's footsteps. He wants to abandon the isolationist aspects of Judaism and to adapt to the society in which he finds himself. Eventually, however, before throwing Aaron out of the house, Moishe manages to make him feel such a painful sense of guilt that the boy reacts desperately. At the end of the story the reader is told that Aaron has changed his name and is left to speculate what will become of him.

Of the three attitudes to cultural identity presented by Thériault, clearly the author, despite his under-standing and admiration of it, is not recommending the standpoint of Moishe, for whom there is no question of adjustment to social realities. Governed by a multitude of restrictions and taboos, the leftovers of adjustment to the realities of an age more than two thousand years in the past, subjected to constant pressures and incon-venience, Moishe's position invites frustration and tragedy. This point is made clear in other Canadian novels besides *Aaron*. One thinks immediately of Abraham in Adele Wiseman's gripping story *The Sacrifice*, which will be discussed at length in another essay, or of the Zeyda in Mordecai Richler's *The Apprenticeship of Duddy Kravitz* and *Son of a Smaller Hero* or the parallel examples of Father Beaubien and the Westmount group in Hugh MacLennan's *Two Solitudes*. The Moishe attitude, then, is that a culture must be preserved simply because it is there. Generally, this attitude is reinforced by a great superstructure of rites, traditions and religious dogma within the culture itself, and, of course, it is the prime cause and sustenance of racist philosophy.

The Moishe attitude thus coincides in essence with the position of Lionel Groulx and the various extremists of English Canada; and when it happens that any culture is preserved unchanged beyond the point of usefulness, then the continuity must be partly attributed to the Moishe way of thinking. I say partly attributed because, as happened in the case of Aaron, excessive coercion to embrace an ideology which is too prohibitive, too far removed from actuality, can very often drive a person to total rejection of it. Or, as happened with the hundreds of thousands of French Canadians who immigrated to

New England, when a static and obsolescent set of values is confronted by a strong, dynamic culture, more favourable to the self-realization of the individual, the result will be complete assimilation into the new culture within two or three generations. Thus when a static culture is maintained without change, the Moishe-Groulx attitude is only partly responsible. Of greater significance is what can perhaps be called the facility for assimilation of surrounding ethnic groups. Ironic as it may seem, the English-Canadian attitude typified by Susanna Moodie, with its exclusiveness and its tendency since the days of Thomas Haliburton to shun the dynamic, has probably done more to preserve French-Canadian culture in North America than the attitude exemplified by Lionel Groulx.

Which brings us to Thériault's second approach to cultural identity, that of Viedna-Cécile. The tone of *Aaron* strongly suggests that the author does not favour Viedna-Cécile's solution. She has decided to become completely assimilated; and to do so she is prepared to deny her true identity. The first weakness in this approach is that it may not work, and Viedna-Cécile will be caught in an ethnic no-man's-land. In another of his poignant short poems, A.M. Klein captures the idea precisely:

Now we will suffer loss of memory:
We will forget the things we must eschew.
We will eat ham, despite our tribe's tabu,
Ham buttered . . . and on fast days . . . publicly . . .
Null, then, and void, the kike nativity.
Our family albums we will hide from view.
Ourselves, we'll do what all pretenders do,
And like the ethnics mightily strive to be.
Our recompense? . . . Emancipation-day!
We will find friend where once we found but foe.
Impugning epithets will glance astray.

To gentile parties we will proudly go;
And Christians, anecdoting us, will say:
"Mr. and Mrs. Klein—the Jews, you know . . ."

The novel *Under the Ribs of Death* by John Marlyn
provides a vivid dramatization of the same idea. Sandor
Hunyadi is ashamed of his Hungarian cultural identity,
and he attempts to submerge it completely. He changes
his name to Alex Hunter. Eventually, however, in a
scene reminiscent of Anton Chekhov, he finds himself
alone staring at a beetle; he is no longer able to join even
the circle of his immediate family. Noah, in Richler's
Son of a Smaller Hero, has a similar experience.

Assimilation, evidently, is a more complicated process
than one would suspect. As I intimated earlier, it can
take place involuntarily when a static culture encounters
a dynamic one. Yet, as Thériault, Klein, Marlyn and a
number of other writers make clear, when an individual
consciously sets out to become assimilated by another
ethnic group, the consequences most likely will be
isolation and demoralizing loss of self-respect. A person
cannot simply dismiss all the habits and associations
which result from emotional involvement with a culture.
Moreover, the great majority of people, it seems, would
never dream of attempting to do so. Assimilation is like
romantic love—it cannot be charted or forced; if it is
going to happen, it will take its own natural course.

Thériault's third approach to cultural identity, that
which Aaron first considers adopting, is both more
simple and more complex than the other two, but to my
mind it is the only intelligent and legitimate approach.
It is a course somewhere in between blind devotion and
total rejection, and it is motivated by the normal human
desire for self-realization. In effect, it is an attempt by
the individual to adapt to the social realities in which he
finds himself without denying his identity. But he must
of necessity abandon those aspects of his ethnic

culture—the taboos, the racist notions of purity and superiority, the inculcated pseudo-religious duty to protect and preserve traditions—which interfere with accommodation to a broad community of human beings.

In other words, the individual must treat culture not as an untouchable mystical force, but as a set of social norms which permit him to be himself, to be part of a special community, and at the same time to live with people who are not of his special community. His self-respect must depend upon himself and his personal achievements rather than upon identification with a culture, and once he comes to that realization he will regard other people accordingly. Reversing the decision of Jules Lantagnac in *L'Appel de la race*, he must put his natural inclinations, his own happiness and that of his dependents, before any duty to protect a cultural mystique. For surely a culture is there to serve people rather than people to serve a culture.

In both *Barometer Rising* and *Two Solitudes*, Hugh MacLennan, the author who has probably examined the problem of Canadian cultural identities more closely than any other, provides a strong tonal endorsement for our third approach. The characters Geoffrey Wain, Marius, Athanase Tallard, Huntly McQueen and Father Beaubien are all warped one way or another by their feelings of obligation to an ethic ideology. Each one is prevented from obeying his natural inclinations. Wain and McQueen are materially successful, but from the human point of view they are grotesque, both given to ruthlessness disguised as duty, Wain finding human contact only in the paid-for embrace of his pitiful little mistress and McQueen sharing his dream mansion on the mountain with a Persian cat and a photograph of his mother. Marius and Father Beaubien stew in their own venom, while old Tallard re-enacts a Greek tragedy. On the other hand, Wain's daughter Penny and her boyfriend Neil free themselves to adjust to life by abandoning the prejudices of the old Halifax society. Yardley, Paul and Heather in *Two Solitudes* also insist upon being themselves rather than the serving vessels of a cultural ideology. And it is clear that Hugh MacLennan presents their attitude as the only acceptable approach to cultural identity in Canada.

But as illustrated in *Two Solitudes* as well as in *Aaron* and *Son of a Smaller Hero*, even for those who see culture in the proper light, there is one major obstacle to uneventful and natural implementation of the third approach—the accusation of being a traitor to one's ethnic group. Moreover, as Lionel Groulx contends in *L'Appel de la race*, once the barrier is lowered just a bit, once the exclusiveness is dropped, total assimilation is sure to follow sooner or later. My answer to Groulx is simply this: whenever there is danger of an ethnic culture disappearing, then there is something seriously wrong with it, and it is ready for the museum case and the social history textbooks. When, to use the Lorenz phrase, a set of social norms and rites are impediments rather than aids to the individual, then it is time for them to be either modified or permitted to die.

In the case of French-Canadian culture, incidentally, the influence of Groulx and his disciples notwithstanding, modification is indeed beginning to take place. From all appearances, the cultural ideology of French Canada is becoming less static, stronger and more practical. It is being put to the test of twentieth-century reality, and the revered traditions *du bon vieux temps*—huge families, classical college education for the élite, distrust of everything foreign and especially of France, pea soup instead of chicken in the pot, the parish priest as a unique link with absolute truth—these traditions have already gone the way of the snows of yesteryear. There is now a strong possibility, indeed a probability, that French Canada, released from the duty of preserving an obsolescent status quo, will emerge with a viable, distinctive and highly dynamic new cultural identity. The phenomenon is reflected in the vigour and variety of recent literary production, in the works of Bessette, Godbout, Carrier, Martin, Blais, Aquin, Ducharme and a number of others, and especially in such novels as Jean Simard's *Mon Fils pourtant heureux* and Richard Joly's *Le Visage de l'attente*, where the customs of the good old days are significantly treated as subject matter for nostalgia rather than as patterns for modern living.

Some of these authors, as I pointed out earlier, also dramatize the frustration and anxiety which are in large part the lingering effects of the old static culture. For the influence of the philosophy of Lionel Groulx can no doubt be more accurately calculated in automobiles wrapped around trees at a hundred miles an hour on antique roads, than in genuine French-Canadian accomplishments. But undoubtedly the most fascinating aspect of the emerging new cultural identity of French Canada is that it may well replace the old group inferiority complex by a sense of confidence, which, coupled with the right attitudes on the part of English Canadians, could lead to a highly satisfactory *modus vivendi* in Canada.

It would appear that attitudes in English-speaking Canada are also being modified. Whereas the racism of French Canada simply perpetuated the vicious circle of racist action and reaction, producing only antipathy, Québec's current "quiet revolution" has aroused a great deal of interest and sympathy. The changes taking place in English Canada are, of course, not quite so dramatic. Having never been homogeneous in the first place, and having always been quite unavoidably affected by the culture of the United States, an awareness of which has too often led to the neurotic pointlessness of anti-Americanism, the English-speaking elements of the Canadian population are now searching for the kind of cultural distinction French Canadians have always had. And ironically enough, if there is indeed the possibility that one of the major ethnic groups of Canada is eventually going to be assimilated by the other, it could well be the new French-Canadian cultural identity which comes out on top. One need only witness the recent frantic rush among English-speaking businessmen in Québec and elsewhere for courses in French conversation, to realize that such a speculation is not entirely groundless.

Whatever might come to pass in the far distant future, however, need not concern us here. Free from stunting racist philosophy, this nation will grow in the natural way that it should, adapting to the exigencies of each successive age. Canada may always have two principal ethnic groups and a variety of other smaller groups, but what all these groups already have in common has in fact created a distinctive, all-embracing Canadian mystique, something independent of and transcending the separate ethnic identities. For as I pointed out in the previous essay, "Twin Solitudes," it can be shown that the major literary works of both English and French Canada share a common spectrum of basic themes.

The problem of ethnic relations, on the other hand, as we observed at the very beginning of this analysis, has so far never been a basic theme of Canadian literature. And perhaps this fact is a good omen. It can be said, nevertheless, that certain Canadian writers have provided insight into the subject of ethnic coexistence. As Susanna Moodie, Lionel Groulx, John Marlyn, Hugh MacLennan, A.M. Klein and Yves Thériault each in his own way makes clear, with regard to cultural identity both fanatical devotion and total rejection are negative attitudes, tending to foster racism, hatred, frustration, isolation or needless discord. These attitudes have existed and continue to exist in Canada, but there are indications, reflected in the more recent of the works examined, that as a nation we are steadily evolving away from the limitations of Lionel Groulx and Susanna Moodie. We are beginning to comprehend the significance of the Rilke lines quoted by Hugh MacLennan in *Two Solitudes* that "Love consists in this, that two solitudes protect, and touch and greet each other." We are rightly not about to lose our separate cultural identities, but we are beginning to realize that the value of any ethnic culture in a nation such as ours can never depend upon its power to isolate people from one another, that Canadian consciousness can be a good deal more than, to use MacLennan's own phrase, "race-memories lonely in great spaces."

The Calvinist-Jansenist Pantomime

Canada did not have the colourful spectacle of Pilgrim
Fathers landing on a rock, but she has certainly proved
more faithful to the Puritan ethos than has the United
States of America. And what is even more significant,
Canadian Puritanism has evolved in much the same way
and has taken much the same form of expression in
Protestant English Canada as in Roman Catholic
Québec.

It is not, of course, all that surprising that English
Canada and French Canada, despite widespread belief to
the contrary and obvious divergences in their respective
major church systems, should share a common fundamental theology. We know that the Protestant religion
in this country was strongly conditioned by Calvinism.
And as a number of historians have pointed out,
French-Canadian Catholicism was influenced by
Jansenism, an essentially Calvinistic doctrine introduced
by Cornelius Jansen, Bishop of Ypres, at the beginning

of the seventeenth century. Based upon predestination and using the rather imaginative, if perhaps a bit sinister symbol of a crucifix with the arms of Christ only partially spread, embracing the "elect" but giving all others the eternal cold shoulder, this doctrine blossomed for a time in Europe and was centered, very suggestively from the Canadian standpoint, in the monastery of Port-Royal, France. Exactly how Jansenism made inroads into French Canada seems still something of a mystery. Did the explorer and colonizer Samuel de Champlain have anything to do with it? Did particular immigrant priests spread the message? How did the unmistakable Jansenist crucifixes—one can yet be seen at the Fort Beauséjour Museum in New Brunswick—get into this country? One thing is certain, that the Jesuits vehemently opposed Jansenism, as eventually did the Vatican itself to the point of Pope Clement XI issuing a condemnatory bull entitled *Unigenitus* in 1713.

The Church's official proscription has undoubtedly had a lot to do with the obscurity surrounding Canadian Jansenism, and with the apparent reluctance on the part of qualified church historians to probe the subject too deeply. Jansenism has been the skeleton in the French-Canadian closet. It is slyly alluded to in novels—"Et la graine janséniste prolifère sur nos terres," in Jean Simard's *Mon Fils pourtant heureux*—and is the subject of bitter poetry—"Le Retour d'Oedipe," by Pierre Trottier. But always one is more aware of its gloomy effects on French-Canadian society than of its precise doctrinal influence upon the Québec church. Of interest to note, however, is that the Jansenist-hating Jesuits, with their emphasis on purifying and simplifying the Christian faith, on scholarship, and on austerity and return to the basic teaching of Jesus (hence the name), were far closer to the Jansenists than the order itself has ever cared to admit. Perhaps there was a measure of professional jealousy involved. Quite possibly the Canadian Jesuits inadvertently fostered certain Jansenist ideas. But whatever the case, the Jansenism of French Canada and the Calvinism of English Canada inculcated exactly the same attitudes regarding man's relationship to God and his role on earth.

These attitudes, echoed in many Canadian literary works and remarked upon frequently in other essays in this volume, can be briefly summarized as follows. Man in himself is insignificant and deserves nothing better than hell unless the grace of God has been bestowed upon him. There is nothing he can do to catch God's eye. Either he has been chosen or he has not. However, the desire, abundantly demonstrated, to attend church regularly and do one's assigned task on earth diligently and without complaint—"la résignation chrétienne"— can be indicative of the prepossession of God's grace. Contrary inclinations, especially idleness and the wish to pursue personal comfort and pleasure, are clear indications of predestined damnation. And an interest in art which is not patently moralistic or didactic is at best highly suspicious. Being after all only flesh and blood, man must be expected to have the occasional fling—a roaring drunk or a roll in the hay—but if he has God's grace in his bones, then the flings must result in misery rather than joy. He must never delude himself into thinking that the so-called sins of the flesh are in any way satisfying. To succumb to the fires of passion is understandable and possibly even excusable, but to enjoy it is the sure sign of different and everlasting fires to come. Saturday night, being followed so closely by Sunday morning and the moment of truth in God's house, is commonly accepted as the most appropriate time for flings. Man's role on earth, then, is to follow the prescribed rules, do his duty and suffer his "purgatoire sur terre" on the strength of a pre-issued, church-stamped passport to heaven.

Now anyone who has examined studies of early American Puritanism will immediately recognize the similarities between it and the Calvinist-Jansenist set of attitudes I have just described, attitudes reflected in the works of Canadian writers. Both rationales, of course, are derived from the Puritan ethos. It should also be noted, however, that between the two there are significant differences of interpretation and degree of emphasis. The major Puritan thinkers of New England put far more stress on the depravity of man and the graphic qualities of the hell they felt he so rightly deserved. Indeed, Jonathan Edwards, the celebrated American preacher, seemed not even satisfied by the thought that most people would go to the traditional hell, and he often occupied his considerable intellect to conceive novel hells of ever-mounting horror. American Puritanism—and this distinction is highly significant— also laid more emphasis upon self-reliance and the responsibility of the individual, for in reaction against an Established Church it insisted that there should be no hierarchical or extensively structured church system. In Canada, by contrast, both Calvinist and Jansenist ideas existed within relatively sophisticated ecclesiastical systems. The American Puritans, moreover, in compensation for the demotion of the ecclesiastical aspects of religion, underlined the notion that any man's work could be holy and that success in any legitimate occupation, including commerce, reflected the presence of divine grace. In *The Protestant Ethic and the Spirit of Capitalism*, Max Weber discusses the import of this principle of the whole recent evolution of Western civilization. Finally, there is the "fling" syndrome. While marked counterparts exist in Scotland and in both Protestant and Catholic Ireland, in North America it seems definitely to be more a Canadian than an American phenomenon. This is undoubtedly because New England Puritanism called so strongly for

individual responsibility, self-examination and commitment, working out one's own salvation "through fear
and trembling." Canadians, on the other hand, always
had the security of reliance upon a church establishment
of one kind or another, upon detailed rules of
behaviour, and upon the near certainty that Sunday
morning would follow Saturday night. In short,
American Puritanism was not satisfied with simple
human discomfort and anxiety. It demanded more than
the normal person was prepared to bear, and that is why
it fell apart.

When compared with the New England variety, then,
Canadian Puritanism has certain differentiating characteristics, although the fact has not been generally
recognized. Commenting on *Each Man's Son* in his book
O Canada, the American critic Edmund Wilson relates
how the Boston publishers of this novel insisted that
Hugh MacLennan add an introduction to explain
Calvinism in Nova Scotia. Wilson goes on to say, "It is
curious, but characteristic of our assumption of the
remoteness of Canada, that any such explanation
should have been thought to be necessary—and, of all
things, an explanation of Calvinism in, of all places,
Boston." (p. 71) In the light of what we have observed
above, however, the action of the Boston publishers was
not so curious. They might well have sensed a peculiar
and distinctive quality about the Calvinistic attitudes
described by MacLennan. Certainly anyone brought up
on the famous works emanating from New England
Puritanism, the novels and stories of Melville and
Hawthorne, would see little thematically in common
with *Each Man's Son*, or with anything else in Canadian
literature for that matter. The closest similarity, aside
from now forgotten minor verse of the colonial period,
is probably found in the long narrative poems of E. J.
Pratt, and not because of any affinity to the Puritan
ethos but because Pratt achieved epic proportions by

reducing opposite forces to a basic duality, which in certain respects corresponds to the Puritan duality of good and evil.

Duality of another kind, however, is the key to the main divergence between the devolution of the Puritan tradition in the United States and its stubborn development in Canada. Nearly two hundred years ago American Puritanism split in two, and that nation has been suffering from philosophical schizophrenia ever since. The split is most clearly seen in the literary careers of two famous men—Jonathan Edwards, the clergyman mentioned earlier, and Benjamin Franklin, diplomat, inventor, by strange circumstance founder of the Montreal *Gazette*, prototype and epitome of the practical, hustling Yankee who gets things done. At first sight this pair would appear to have nothing in common, but literary critics in the United States have convincingly shown how Franklin exemplifies the Puritan tradition as much in his own way as does Edwards in his. What Franklin accomplished was to take the principles of industry, self-organization, self-reliance and success as signals of God's grace, then more or less drop God from the scheme. The branch he thus broke from the Puritan tree quickly sprouted roots and has grown to towering proportions. And having abandoned the Puritan God, the materialist tradition of the United States has invented a succession of its own deities, from Irving's "almighty dollar" to the status symbol. Meanwhile, Jonathan Edwards went to the opposite extreme, moving further and further away from the pragmatism of the Pilgrim Fathers, tormenting himself with the impossible task of harmonizing dark Calvinism with enlightened rationalism, and inaugurating a tradition of highly disciplined intellectualism. This tradition has also flowered in the United States. It too, of course, soon dropped the old Puritan God, had already done so by the time of Emerson and Thoreau, but it has retained an obsession with ethical and moral issues. Of special interest is how this American artist-intellectual tradition, in reaction to the increasing conformism of the materialist stream, has elevated and glorified the principle of individual self-reliance, the capacity and the right of a person to think for himself.

Awareness of a fundamental dichotomy, I might add, has always been a powerful motivating and conditioning force in American literature. Tension between two magnetic poles, between a distorted group view and a natural individual view of life, characterizes all the great literary works of the United States. Melville's *Moby Dick* places the old Puritan preoccupation with sin and the resultant compulsion to see all things as either good or evil against the simple desire to live, let live and learn about life as it is. By the time of Mark Twain's *Huckleberry Finn*, the two parallel streams have become more defined and the tension has resolved into the opposing pulls of a materialistic, morally decadent society and the will of natural man to act upon his natural impulses. A major novel of contemporary American literature, Ken Kesey's *One Flew Over the Cuckoo's Nest*, again presents natural man, wanting like Ishmael and Huck Finn only to live, let live and act according to his personal impulses, but this time he is confronted with a gigantic, thoroughly regimented system (ingeniously represented by Kesey as a state insane asylum). It is perhaps an ominous note that whereas the protagonists of Melville and Twain survive, Kesey's hero is finally crushed by the system (again ingeniously), although the narrator, like Ishmael, does manage to escape in the end.

Canadian literature, understandably, has not been dominated by a tension between two opposite poles, for as we have observed, the Canadian Puritan ethos was never as intense as the American, and it has never split in two. Consequently, Canada did not witness the emergence of the two extremes of materialism and intellectual-individualism, and the proximity of the United States provided a safety valve against anyone who happened to develop a taste for one or other of the extremes. Canadian churches, as I have already suggested, have been careful not to risk cutting their own throats by encouraging intellectual self-reliance. The stress, in fact, was evidently placed upon the human-insignificance-and-impotence part of the Puritan ideology, making man more than ever dependent upon the church institution as custodian of God's grace. The artist or intellectual operating outside of the ethical framework has remained to this day something of a dubious character here, someone to be leery of. Schools and publishing houses in particular have suffered from the stifling grip of direct or indirect church control—the idea of neutral schools in Québec, beyond any rational doubt the ideal solution for all concerned, is still regarded by the majority of people as the blackest of heresies. While the great split had the effect of releasing Americans from the restrictive aspects of the old Puritan theology, Canadians have largely remained enslaved, uninspired to move wholeheartedly one way or the other. That is one of the main reasons why Canada, compared to the United States, has never produced within her boundaries a proportionately impressive intellectual-artistic élite or a proportionately efficient business machine. In Canadian literature, from Haliburton through Leacock, Ringuet and MacLennan, to the recent hodge-podge of essays called *The New Romans*, edited by Al Purdy, the American duality has always produced a duality of reaction—admiration for American accomplishment and fear of American licence and extremism. Sam Slick, the successful Yankee trader, is at once admirable and despicable. But the one thing he most definitely is not, is Canadian. No wonder the Americans think of Haliburton as the father of

American humour.

The Calvinist-Jansenist ethos of Canada, then, did not undergo a dramatic transmogrification. It has, nevertheless, slowly evolved, growing a bit senile and toothless with age, but still snarling in the second half of the twentieth century. Canadian literature has mirrored this evolution, in the religious-passion novels of Laure Conan and the early propaganda tracts of Antoine Gérin-Lajoie and Ralph Connor, then in the *roman du terroir* or novels of the soil of Hémon, Grove, Ringuet and a host of others. The modern tendency, which actually began in some of the novels of the soil and in the naturalistic works of Albert Laberge, is to reflect the lingering effects of the Puritan ethos as a kind of psycho-philosophical hangover which if it is not a peculiarly Canadian phenomenon, certainly has a special Canadian flavour. Women writers in particular—Anne Hébert, Claire Martin, Ethel Wilson, Marie-Claire Blais, Margaret Laurence, Suzanne Paradis—seem drawn to this mental condition. It provides, of course, unlimited tragic possibilities for unfulfilled and thwarted romantic love, an aspect of Canadian literature which was noted with some fascination by Edmund Wilson, the American critic. But as I mentioned earlier, it is not surprising that modern American readers in general should not immediately grasp all the implications of MacLennan's *Each Man's Son.* Nor perhaps would they find Roch Carrier's *La Guerre, yes sir!* completely intelligible. These two novels, similar in many respects, describe a state of mind probably unfamiliar to commonplace modern American experience. The fact that they have both appeared in the second half of the twentieth century must in itself cause a certain amount of wonder and bafflement.

For Canadian readers, on the other hand, *Each Man's Son* and *La Guerre, yes sir!* are dealing with things as familiar as pea soup and snow storms. MacLennan's Dr.

Ainslie struggling with his feelings of guilt, making himself suffer for his legitimate and normal desires, and for his presumed failures, fearing happiness—all of it is quite standard. The "fling" syndrome is vividly illustrated in the book by the miners drinking themselves senseless on a Saturday night, then dragging their hangovers to church on Sunday morning. Carrier's *La Guerre* has many parallels. The main event of the story is a riotous wake to celebrate the return of the body of a soldier killed in the war. Throughout the wake, chanted prayers alternate with magnificent curses, full-throated, juicy curses exactly of a kind with those of MacLennan's coal miners, or of Robert Kroetsch's hero in *Words of My Roaring*—"Calice de ciboire d'hostie! Christ en bicyclette sur son Calvaire. Gros tas de merde debout!" (p. 77). The blasphemies, naturally, are derived from the liturgy of the church, as if the suppressed spirit of man were hurling defiance at the instrument of its suppression in a jargon certain to be understood. I strongly suspect that cursing in the best Calvinist-Jansenist tradition has a virulence and intensity all of its own.

La Guerre, yes sir! includes a good example of the terror sermon, delivered by a parish priest at the burial service for the dead soldier. It is typical that this sermon should contain several threatening allusions to sins of the flesh, for undoubtedly sex relations have been more greatly distorted by the Puritan ethos than has any other area of human activity. Here again there would appear to be a particular Canadian Calvinist-Jansenist flavour. In American literature and in other literatures are found many works describing reaction to Puritan restrictions. But this reaction, such as in Hawthorne's *The Scarlet Letter*, is generally a positive and satisfying act of defiance. The tendency in Canadian literature seems to lean in the direction of impotence and incapacity to act, or an impetuous and foolish action entirely devoid of satisfaction. One thinks of George and the young Catherine in Hugh MacLennan's *The Watch That Ends the Night*, of Niels Lindstedt and Clara in Grove's *Settlers of the Marsh*, of Pierre, Denis and Fernande in Lemelin's *Pierre le magnifique*, of Philip Bentley and the choir girl in Sinclair Ross' *As For Me and My House*, of Alexander MacDonald and Ellen in Hugh Hood's *White Figure, White Ground*, of Anne Hébert's characters and a host of others in French-Canadian and English-Canadian fiction. Carrier's *La Guerre, yes sir!* provides an excellent parody of this kind of reaction in its description of the soldier Bérubé's first meeting with a Newfoundland prostitute:

> Bérubé feverishly tore off his jacket, then sat on the bed to unbutton his shirt. He was trembling; he had the sensation that the bed was charged with electricity . . . .
> The girl was standing in front of him, almost nude. She had kept on her brassiere, filled to the point of bursting. She held out her arms to Bérubé. But he was not able to get up, to leap toward this naked girl, to take her in his arms, hug her violently, then toss her on the bed. He felt completely feeble, as if he had had too much to drink. In his head he heard a tick-tock like the beating of a drum. "FOREVER-NEVER" repeated this monstrous clock which had marked the passing hours of his childhood, the clock of hell announcing for all eternity "FOREVER-NEVER"—the damned are in hell FOREVER, they will escape NEVER. Under the clock Bérubé saw serpents entwined in ever-lasting flames creeping through slimy caverns, and he saw the damned, naked, strangling among the flames and the serpents. "FOREVER-NEVER" ticked the clock of his child-hood, the clock of eternal damnation for those who bared their flesh and for those who dallied with

naked women. "FOREVER-NEVER" sounded the
clock, and Bérubé could not hold back the words:
"Do you want to marry me?"
"Yes," replied the girl, to whom no-one had ever
before posed the question.
"What's your name?"
"Molly."[11]

In Frederick Philip Grove's *Settlers of the Marsh*,
there is a proposal under very similar circumstances, but
presented in deadly serious manner when Niels
Lindstedt's Puritan conscience will not permit him to do
otherwise once he has slept with the prostitute Clara.

Perhaps the most obvious distinguishing characteristic
of the effect of the Calvinist-Jansenist ideology on
Canadian literature, however, lies in the portrayal of
clergymen by Canadian writers. To begin with, surely
there are more clergymen per book in Canadian
literature than in the literature of any other country.
Not only Canadian writers, but foreign writers who have
sojourned in this country and then written books seem
to have been compelled to underline the relatively
extraordinary position of the priest or minister in
Canadian society—Louis Hémon and Sara Jeannette
Duncan are examples, but probably the best illustration
is the novel *Napoleon Tremblay*, written by the Scot
Angus Graham. It is, however, not so much the
frequency of the clergyman in Canadian literature, but
rather the nature of the characterizations which constitutes the real distinction. I have already observed that
in contrast to the recurring principle of individual
self-reliance in American society and literature, Canadian society has always exemplified the dependent
relationship of man to an established church system.
There is no need for me to enumerate the books
which favourably dramatize this relationship—they are
legion. In both French and English Canada there has

also been a strong subcultural folklore tradition of bawdy songs and tales presenting clergymen as secret degenerates or comic philanderers. Whenever this folk tradition has come to the surface, such as in Rodolphe Girard's *Marie Calumet*, a novel published in 1904 which describes the rivalry of two rustics for the favours of their curé's housekeeper, and other unseemly antics in the presbytery, there has been an explosion of public indignation. It's quite all right to sing dirty songs after a drink or two at a party, but damned is he who does the same sort of thing in print—at least that is the way it was until recently. In the case of Girard, the Québec journal *La Vérité* went so far as to accuse him of the then ultimate degradation—Freemasonry!—the equivalent of being communist today. Girard, I might add as a matter of record, immediately slapped a libel suit on the publishers and, curiously enough, won his case. *La Vérité* had strayed from *la vérité*. Whether favourably or unfavourably portrayed, however, the dominant presence of the clergyman in Canadian creative works is a clear indication of the special impact of the church on Canadian consciousness.

The Calvinist-Jansenist texture of this impact is best illustrated by the remarkably frequent theme of the *prêtre manqué*, a term which I am going to use broadly to mean both the would-be clergyman and the clergyman who for some reason cannot fit into the established ecclesiastical pattern; in other words, "the imperfect priest." Perhaps a more exact term would be *hérétique manqué*, but it is unfamiliar and unwieldy. Actually *prêtre manqué* has come to connote exactly the mental attitude of frustration and guilt that I wish to explore, and if one is willing to restrict the word *prêtre* to signify only a total and unquestioning acceptance of doctrine, then one may allow that even a clergyman may be a *prêtre manqué*. Conversely, a clergyman who rejects doctrine but remains in his ministry, as often seems to

74

happen these days, and has no feelings of guilt or anxiety about his position, is not a *prêtre manqué*. For the expression means someone who deeply regrets that he cannot be the perfect priest.

A characteristic feature of the Canadian *prêtre manqué* is that he does not try to attack or destroy the institution to which he cannot adjust. In fact, he rarely attempts even to break away from that institution. Instead he suffers personal torment, searching his soul to find out what his own deficiency must be, and more often than not he ends up finding a *modus vivendi*, however fragile, through some device of self-effacing adaptation. Which, of course, accords precisely with the anti-self-reliance, human-insignificance emphasis mentioned earlier in connection with the distinctive flavour of Canadian Puritanism.

Morley Callaghan's *Such is My Beloved* and Gilles Marcotte's *Le Poids de Dieu* are probably the best dramatizations of the *prêtre manqué* as defined above, in Canadian literature. *As For Me and My House*, by Sinclair Ross, is another excellent study. Its protagonist, the Reverend Philip Bentley, continues for many years to practise a ministry in which he does not believe, or at least cannot fully accept. But he lacks the confidence and determination necessary to break away, and he spends his time sitting at his desk sketching people without faces (absence of self-reliant individualism?) and the false store fronts of his sterile little prairie town. When finally his frustration and convenient opportunity lead him to seduce an infatuated and equally frustrated choir girl, the act is not a grand passion, not even an expression of affection or physical desire. It is an empty and self-punishing gesture, its punishment further heightened by adoption of the resultant illegitimate child. The adoption, in fact, is doubly punishing, for Bentley's wife, who knows the circumstances, agrees to go through with it in order to chastise herself. Bentley's struggle is thus essentially interior. There is no question of open confrontation with the institution or the hypocrisies associated with it. His dream, which the book suggests may possibly be realized eventually, is to withdraw quietly to a bookstore business.

In André Langevin's *Le Temps des hommes* the dénouement is likewise a withdrawal. The central character, a priest called Pierre Dupas, gives up his ministry after he witnesses a child die of spinal meningitis. He can no longer accept the Calvinist-Jansenist tenet that this innocent child, if not among those elected to God's grace, is automatically sentenced to eternal damnation. Moreoever, and this point is typical, he feels guilty because he has dared to challenge established doctrine. And what does he do? He goes off into the forest and lives a life of deprivation and solitude. Roger Lemelin's *Pierre le magnifique* supplies a little more variety. After he has been put through a seminary by a kindly old priest, Pierre Boisjoly rejects the idea of taking holy orders. Eventually he finds himself alone with the woman he loves, Fernande. The two declare their love to each other passionately, and the reader says to himself, "This is it." But it isn't. In fact, the episode leads Pierre to decide on the priest-hood after all. I should perhaps repeat here that I am using the notion of *prêtre manqué* to include those who actually become clergymen (like Pierre, and like the priest in Richard Joly's *Le Visage de l'attente* or Padre Doorn in McDougall's *Execution*, to give two other examples), those who fail to do so (like the hero of Jean-Paul Pinsonneault's *Jérôme Aquin* or Latendresse in MacLennan's *Return of the Sphinx*), and those who do so and then backtrack (like Bentley and Dupas). The criterion is a person's state of mind rather than his position in life, a state of mind marked by appre-hensions which lead to retreat, self-effacing adaptation and self-punishment instead of a frontal attack upon the religious institution.

Morley Callaghan and Gilles Marcotte, as I have said, provide the most penetrating analyses of the *prêtre manqué*, and examination of these two character studies brings to light another of the notable parallels between Canadian literature in French and Canadian literature in English. Both Father Dowling of *Such is My Beloved* and Abbé Savoie of *Le Poids de Dieu* begin as young priests with highly idealized visions of the sacerdotal role they will enact in their ministries. Both are intellectually inclined, gentle, hypersensitive and intrigued by the religious mystique. But contrary to their expectations, Dowling and Savoie soon find a panorama of sordid realities when they are assigned to churches in working-class districts. God may still be in his heaven, but nothing is right with the world. In both books there is an identical tension between the young crusading priest (Savoie and Dowling share a passion for reforming the world) and the hard-headed practical clergymen with whom they must work. Confronted with real-life problems, both Dowling and Savoie become pitifully entangled and are never even close to finding solutions. When he is called upon to settle a workers' strike, Abbé Savoie proves hopelessly ineffectual. He acts courageously and impetuously in blessing the engagement of an adolescent girl and boy without the approval of either his superiors or the parents, then flees in panic when the young girl, suffering from tuberculosis, takes a fit of coughing. Father Dowling is more willing to enter the dark lives of his parishioners than is Abbé Savoie, but his well-intentioned efforts are equally ineffectual, if not actually detrimental to the welfare of the people involved. Being prevented by doctrine from advising the desperate mother of too many children that she should have the common sense to practise birth control, he must fall back on the barren plea for "Christian resignation to a life of misery." After the initial shock of being propositioned by two young whores as he is walking along the street with his clerical collar hidden by a scarf, Father Dowling starts a long campaign to save the girls. He gives them money, buys them gifts, attempts to find them jobs, even succeeds in winning their confidence—which is quite an accomplishment, considering that the closest either of the girls has come to genuine male concern for her welfare has been with a pimp. But the whole affair falls through when the girls are run out of town through the intervention of the local bishop, who fears that a scandal would ruin his current charity drive and tarnish the image of the church. And the bishop, of course, is quite right. Obviously it will not do to have a priest spending too much time with prostitutes—how are people to know that the motivation lies in his profession and not in that of the girls? Like Abbé Savoie, Father Dowling acts naively and in a manner inconsistent with established church policy, placing a little too much confidence in his personal judgement and will. But both young clergymen pay dearly for their indiscretions. In keeping with the character of the *prêtre manqué*, Savoie and Dowling react to failure and censure not by defiance, not by an attack upon a system which each has found inadequate, but by withdrawing into a state of profound depression. Each man undergoes the familiar process of tormented soul-searching (much better documented by Marcotte than by Callaghan), seeking the personal deficiency which will explain the tension between the institution and himself. And predictably, both Abbé Savoie and Father Dowling eventually arrive at the self-effacing accommodation so characteristic of the Canadian Calvinist-Jansenist tradition.

Neither man, it should be noted, appears to derive any real satisfaction from the final accommodation. Each remains essentially a *prêtre manqué*, unable to fit perfectly into the system but willing to suffer the subordination of his own being to the presumed greater aims of the church. "Le message de l'Eglise n'est pas compromis par ces misères," concludes Abbé Savoie. He also appears to detect in the end that the concept of God which has been inculcated in him has a particular colouring, a distinctive Calvinist-Jansenist colouring we are now in a position to suggest—"A certain idea of God, which is not God," says Savoie, "but the most subtle distortion of Him, lies in me like a deep wound, a wound inflicted so long ago and suffered for such a long time that I am unable to heal it."[12] Consequently, the only thing to do is to suffer it. Father Dowling goes even further, speculating that his suffering may be offered as a kind of sacrifice for Ronnie and Midge, the two prostitutes whose lives he has succeeded only in making more miserable than they were:

> And in the quiet room, he wondered where the two girls were, and what had become of them; they were among the living, they were moving among those who slowly passed before him, all those restless souls the world over who were struggling and dying and finding no peace; he thought with sudden joy that if he would offer up his insanity as a sacrifice to God, maybe God might spare the girls their souls. (p. 287)

It is significant that both Savoie and Dowling depart in one way from the Puritan ethos in its purest, most austere form—each seems to recognize something distasteful about the emphasis on original sin and predestined damnation. Savoie speaks of the distorted idea of God, and Dowling obviously feels there is hope that the two girls may yet be saved by sacrifice. Perhaps it is because of this possibility of stretching the original doctrine that the Canadian Puritan ideology has not collapsed in the way that the American did. Whatever the case, this country's Calvinist-Jansenist tradition, whether in English Protestant, Irish Catholic or French Catholic context, whether officially recognized or officially denied, whether conscious or unconscious, has certainly been stamped by the power to hold onto its own. Instead of rebels, it has produced *prêtres manqués.* And the phenomenon of the *prêtre manqué* remains a widespread and peculiar feature of Canadian literature in both languages.

Finally, I come to what I regard as the "Calvinist-Jansenist Pantomime" of Canadian Letters. This drama, performed in two acts nine years apart, focuses not so much on the content of works of literature as on the treatment two works in particular—Frederick Philip Grove's *Settlers of the Marsh* and Jean-Charles Harvey's *Les Demi-civilisés*—received in Canada. It is surely an accolade to the remarkable staying power of Canadian Puritanism that these two relatively innocent novels, a generation after *Sister Carrie* and *Maggie*, and two generations or more after *Nana* and *Madame Bovary*, should have aroused such shock and censure.

Settlers of the March was published in 1925. Grove himself describes the reaction to it in his alleged autobiography *In Search of Myself.* There is now considerable doubt about much of what Grove relates of his early life in this book, but his description of the effect of *Settlers* seems entirely authentic:

Its publication became a public scandal. Libraries banned it—London, Ontario, forming an honourable exception; reviewers called it "filthy"— W. T. Allison, over the radio; Lorne Pierce nearly lost his job over it; people who had been ready to lionize me cut me dead in the street. As a trade proposition the book never had a chance; what sale it had was surreptitious. I resented this: it was the old story of Flaubert's

Madame Bovary over again. A serious work of art was
classed as pornography; but with this difference that
the error, in Flaubert's case, increased the sales; he
lived in France. In my case, and in Canada, it killed
them. (p. 381)

Jean-Charles Harvey's *Les Demi-civilisés*, published in
March of 1934, achieved the distinction of being banned
by His Eminence Cardinal Villeneuve, of Québec City.
"Son décret," writes Harvey in the Introduction to the
recent re-issue of his book, "publié dans La Semaine
Religieuse, défendait aux fidèles, sous peine de péché
mortel, de lire ce livre, de le garder, prêter, acheter,
vendre, imprimer ou diffuser de quelque façon"—forbade
the faithful, under pain of mortal sin, to read, keep,
loan, buy, print or distribute the book in any way.
Shortly afterwards Harvey lost his job as editor-in-chief
of *Le Soleil* because of the book. Through government
connections he had the chance to become a provincial
librarian, provided he could get the written recommendation of an influential cleric. He immediately went
to see his friend Canon Chamberland, director of
l'Action Catholique, who promised him the reference,
provided the Cardinal did not object. The latter, quotes
Harvey, gave Canon Chamberland the following
instructions: "Faites savoir au premier ministre que je
n'ai aucune objection à ce qu'il confie à M. Harvey
toutes les fonctions qu'il voudra . . . sauf la bibliothèque."—give him anything you like. . .except the
library. And as Harvey goes on to say in the
Introduction:

De là ce compromis: à la bibliothèque, M. Taschereau
nomma le colonel Marquis, statisticien depuis vingt
ans, et, à Harvey, écrivain et journaliste depuis
toujours, il confia la statistique. Le premier ne
connaissait rien aux livres et le second ignorait tout

de la statistique. (p. 10)

In 1937 when the government changed, the new premier, Maurice Duplessis, never a man given to unnecessary subtlety, simply told Jean-Charles Harvey to get out of town.

Now we have already discussed what it was about Canadian society which set the scene for the kind of treatment the books of Grove and Harvey received, even at such a late date. The lingering might of the Calvinist-Jansenist ideology is sufficient explanation. But what was in the books themselves to incur the wrath of the guardians of Puritan morality?

Settlers of the Marsh is Frederick Philip Grove at his best. The story tells of a young Swede who comes to Canada with the dream of a piece of land "with a house of his own and a wife that would go through it like an inspiration." Well he gets the land and the house all right, through hard labour and determination, and he also gets a wife, but her inspirational value, unfortunately, amounts to arousing him to the point of murdering her. Actually Niels Lindstedt is just another character in Canadian fiction whose love relations are distorted by puritanical values. The girl he really wants for his wife and who also loves him, Ellen Amundsen, has witnessed her mother brutalized by her severe, deeply religious father, and she makes a vow never to marry. On the rebound, entirely confounded, Niels has a sexual encounter with the prostitute Clara Vogel, and his Puritan views make it necessary for him to propose marriage. After the usual torment and self-punishment, during which the equally tormented Clara reverts to her old habits, Niels kills her.

Grove's offense in *Settlers of the Marsh* was first that he should have elaborated the "filthy" aspects of the animal nature of man and secondly that he should have suggested that human beings deserve some sort of

satisfaction and happiness on earth, adding the further
suggestion that certain religious attitudes can prevent
and distort this happiness. That Niels, after his release
from prison, and Ellen, after renouncing her vow,
should find a vestige of happiness together in the end,
made Grove's offence even greater. Like the bishop in
Callaghan's *Such is My Beloved*, the indoctrinated
Canadian public of 1925 was not prepared to admit the
existence of sordid realities by according them
attention.

Harvey's *Demi-civilisés* is a clearer case than *Settlers
of the Marsh*. This book openly questions certain
practices of the Church, the government and the law
profession and, depravity of depravities, calmly asserts
that premarital intercourse can be a pleasure. The
book's protagonist, Max Hubert, comes from a rural
community and is described as a mixture of Norman,
Marseillais, Scottish Highlander and Indian. He has
something of the *prêtre manqué*. As a child he wanted
to become a priest, but he is troubled by dreams and by
the cynical remarks of an old man he has befriended.
And, as Harvey puts it, he has " un immense désir de
savoir, au lieu de croire." (p. 38) The book makes clear
that in the author's opinion no Québec institution is
prepared to satisfy that desire, including the University
of Laval—"Si jamais vous entrez là," a professor
tells Max, "ne soyez pas trop frondeur, pas trop
indépendant. Tout ce qui peut ressembler à
l'indépendance de caractère, à l'émancipation de
certains principes, est banni de l'université, gardienne de
la tradition. . . et de la vérité." (p. 47) Through the rich
father of a girl friend, Dorothée Meunier, Max is
eventually set up as editor of an outspoken journal. His
troubles begin when he writes honest criticism of the
work of a revered and mediocre author of the earnest-
thought school. But he weathers that storm and
continues his adventure in Québec City society, giving

Harvey a chance to poke fun at a variety of things. The following passage is an explicit illustration of the "fling syndrome" mentioned earlier in this essay:

> One night Herman got Lucien and me invited to a "wild party" at the Pinon's place. What is a "wild party"? A kind of orgy for little groups of middle-class types, where they really let themselves go—eating, drinking and even making love. These community honeymoons usually take place on the weekend, between 10 o'clock on Saturday night and seven o'clock Sunday morning, so that they can all go to church and erase the sins of the night before.[13]

Harvey is careful to note the trans-Canada nature of the Calvinist-Jansenist influence. "Nous avons des affinités," he points out, "avec les puritains de Toronto, qui pèchent en jouant au bridge le dimanche, mais qui ne se feront pas scrupule de passer cette journée ivres au fond d'une chambre, volets clos." (p. 134)—they regard it as sinful to play bridge on Sunday, but have no scruples about spending the day dead drunk behind closed doors.

Harvey gets in a number of sharp digs at the ignorance of Canadians with regard to culture and art. He tells, for instance, of a member of parliament who "recevant d'Europe une copie de la Vénus de Milo, poursuivit [sued] la compagnie de transport pour avoir cassé et perdu les deux bras de la déesse." (p. 118) Speaking of Québec history, Harvey presents the "Negro King" theory—protection and cultivation of a colonial chief by the dominant foreign power so that he will keep his own people in a servile state—long before the idea was labelled and popularized by André Laurendeau in *Le Devoir*. (pp. 121-2) He severely criticizes the long-established French-Canadian custom (and English-Canadian too) of glorifying the past to the detriment of progress, of hiding "sous notre histoire comme des marmots humiliés [shame-faced brats] sous la jupe de leur mère." (p. 140)

Max Hubert, the protagonist of *Les Demi-civilisés*, has his day of reckoning when one of his collaborators in the journal writes a piece about religion, contending that the organized church has vilified the true message of Christ. In effect this statement is analogous to the feelings which disturb Callaghan's Father Dowling and Marcotte's Abbé Savoie, and the reaction of the authorities is similar. Even those who are sympathetic to the idea are conditioned to shun anything that might rock the ecclesiastical boat. The author of the offending article, a Frenchman, is attacked in the street by a mob called the "Ligue de Moralité," whose members are brandishing a large placard with the words "Aimez-vous les uns les autres." It is significant that the article's author should be a Frenchman rather than a Canadian. It is also significant that he should be rescued from the mob by another colleague, a quiet, powerful French Canadian of peasant stock.

Harvey's novel ends in glaring melodrama when Dorothée, clad in the bridal dress she was to wear for the religious ceremoney of taking the veil as a nun, escapes from the convent and crawls through a snow storm to Max's house She has decided that she would rather have him for a bridegroom than Jesus Christ.

There is no mystery, then, about the nature of Harvey's literary misdemeanours in the eyes of the clerical authorities. If Frederick Philip Grove bares too many unpleasant realities and implies that Puritan values can distort life and love, Jean-Charles Harvey goes a step further in baring a few pleasant realities. He celebrates, with much too obvious a chuckle of delight, naked female flesh and uninhibited sexual relations. He denounces what he aptly calls "une sorte de castration morale" and pinpoints the flaws and the hypocrisy in the

church-orientated society around him. Then to have the
heroine, after tasting the joys of physical embrace,
abandon a holy calling and struggle through a raging
blizzard to taste more—*that* was the final straw.

Yet nowhere in his novel does Harvey attack the basic
principles of religion itself, and certainly one of the
most striking qualities of both *Les Demi-civilisés* and
Settlers of the Marsh for the contemporary reader is the
honesty and sincerity of their authors' intentions. By
modern standards, both books are pristine innocence.
Even by the standards of works which had appeared in
other countries a quarter century or more before them,
these books are mild indeed. One wonders how the
Canadian establishment would have reacted to a local
Becky Sharp or Sister Carrie hustling her body to the
top of the heap. Looking back, the way in which both
Settlers of the Marsh and *Les Demi-civilisés* were
treated, although understandable in the light of the
attitudes we have examined, can only be regarded as
Canadian literature's Calvinist-Jansenist Pantomime.

There is, however, an important epilogue to this
drama. Both *Settlers of the Marsh* and *Les Demi-civilisés*
have been uneventfully re-issued in the 1960s; in fact,
by curious coincidence both in 1966. Obviously Canada
has at last shaken loose from the bonds of Calvinist-
Jansenist captivity at its worst. It was bound to happen
for as we have seen there has long been an awareness of
the particular deformation of life brought about by the
Canadian Puritan ethos, even if this awareness did not
lead to open revolt. In England the story is told of a
Canadian soldier called Jocko who once went on a
church parade with the other members of his military
unit. The soldiers, in full combat gear, marched into the
church and stacked their rifles in one of the aisles before
taking their places in the pews. The service proceeded in
the usual manner until the preacher began to read the
Ten Commandments. It was during this reading that

Jocko threw his crude imitation of a lightning bolt. "Thou shalt not kill—My Arse!" shouted the Canadian soldier. "What are all those bloody guns there for?" And he was duly escorted from the church by military policemen.

A number of Canadians such as Rodolphe Girard, Frederick Philip Grove and Jean-Charles Harvey, have been, as it were, escorted from the church. But their gestures, like Jocko's, have not gone entirely unnoticed. Nor have they been entirely ineffectual. Perhaps in the long run it may prove an advantage that Canada as a nation has been reluctant to undertake a full-scale onslaught upon her established institutions. Such attacks, as we have so often seen in recent years, usually have one of two results: either they succeed in destroying and leave a wreckage of indirection and new extremism, or they arouse a backlash of ultra-conservatism, forcing sympathetic moderates out of the picture, causing outmoded ideas to become more entrenched than ever and actually setting back progress towards an enlightened point of view.

Canada, of course, has not escaped a sense of existential indirection and a degree of extremism, as can readily be seen by examination of much of the best literature produced here since World War II (and discussed at length in other essays in this volume). Nor is this country without a right-wing backlash, although mercifully spared anything comparable to the messianic declamations and sadly effective interventions of a Senator McCarthy, an Enoch Powell or a John Birch Society. The sense of indirection is an inevitable result of the disintegration of traditional values and is more or less a universal phenomenon; the legacy of the long-enduring Canadian Calvinist-Jansenist ethos, it would seem, is that the current sense of indirection is more deeply felt, has a more demoralizing and frustrating effect in Canada than in many other nations. On the other hand, extremism, both right-wing and otherwise, has been relatively limited in this country, especially in comparison to the United States, the nations of Central and South America, France, Ireland, Germany and even Britain. Canadians, like so many of the fictional characters we have looked at, would rather fume than fight. There has been no great division into two opposing camps. The extremists are in tiny minority groups, sometimes fanatical and terrorist, but generally more comical than anything else. Certainly there can be no question that any of these groups speaks for a large segment of the population, as was demonstrated by the general support given to the declaration of the War Measures Act and by the overwhelming vote received by Montreal's Mayor Jean Drapeau after the F.L.Q. terrorist acts of 1970.

Instead of drastic upheaval, suppressive reactionary ideology in Canada has been subjected to a process of slow erosion, and this process may yet prove the best means to improving the human spiritual condition. Of late it has sometimes been fostered from within the erstwhile guardian institutions themselves, by ministers and priests such as Frère Pierre Jérôme (Desbiens) in his *Insolences du Frère Untel*. This book in fact says little that had not been said long before by people such as Jean-Charles Harvey, but Harvey was on the outside. Frère Jérôme, like some of the characters in the books we have examined, did disappear for a time. But then he returned to be appointed a prominent member of the Québec Ministry of Education! Canada has come a long way since Harvey was denied the job of government librarian in the 1930s. The hangover from the strong brew of Canadian Puritanism will undoubtedly be with us for some time yet, both in life and in literature, but there is little likelihood of a repeat performance of the Calvinist-Jansenist Pantomime.

Children of the Changing Wind

It is curious that two of the most impressive adult novels in Canadian literature should be written primarily from the point of view of a child. I am referring, of course, to W. O. Mitchell's *Who Has Seen the Wind* and Réjean Ducharme's *L'Avalée des avalés*.

To avoid any misunderstanding, I should perhaps underline the distinction between books about children, of which there are countless thousands, and books whose authors have specifically adopted the technique of telling a story from a child's viewpoint. So far as I can determine, every published literature of the world contains numerous examples of the first category—books with children as characters. Moreover there is a vast quantity of juvenile fiction, as opposed to adult fiction, and many of these stories have child narrators. The viewpoint of an adolescent or youth, such as Mark Twain's Huckleberry Finn and J. D. Salinger's Holden Caulfield, is also quite common. By contrast, fiction presented from the point of view of a young child is rare indeed, and for obvious reasons. What a child sees is limited in every respect. His interests are strictly emotional and largely predictable—he wants love, food, comfort and fun; and he cannot be expected to comprehend what have long been considered the significant moral and philosophical issues of the human condition. This very innocence of children has afforded many literary opportunities of humour and irony, but usually in poems, short stories or episodes and almost never as the main feature of a successful major work of art intended for adult readers. Accordingly, the fact that Canadian literature should have two such works of art, each a major novel and each a veritable *tour de force* of the sub-genre, is a curious, if not an extraordinary phenomenon.

As a matter of fact, Canadian literature has several examples of this sub-genre, although the other works are all minor compared to *Who Has Seen the Wind* and *L'Avalée des avalés*. In particular one thinks of some of the troubled fiction of Marie-Claire Blais. Her *Manuscrits de Pauline Archange* creates, albeit conditioned by the process of an adult remembering, a world seen through the eyes of a girl about nine or ten years of age. As in most of Blais's works, this world is black and bitter, peopled by cripples, mutes, epileptics and other unfortunates. Similar worlds have been created by the imitators of Réjean Ducharme, such as Victor-Lévy Beaulieu in his painfully obvious *Mémoires d'outre-tonneau*. And Ducharme, with a little more success perhaps, has taken to imitating himself, in *Le Nez qui voque* and *L'Océantume*. The latter is narrated by a youngster called Iode Ssouvie, who lives on a boat christened "Mange de la Merde" with a hard drinking mother and a foreign step-father—essentially the familiar pattern of *L'Avalée des avalés*, which to my mind remains Ducharme's major accomplishment.

And speaking of familiar patterns, before we proceed
to a comparative analysis of *L'Avalée* and *Who Has Seen
the Wind*, two preliminary general observations about
the child in Canadian literature are worthy of mention.
The first concerns something peculiar to French Canada.
Regardless of whether or not he has adopted a child's
point of view, either partially or wholly, or whether the
book deals partly as in a flashback or exclusively with
children, almost every significant French-Canadian
author appears to see childhood with one dominant
characteristic—misery. Over and over again one
encounters fictional children who are unloved,
frustrated, restricted and tormented. The nature and
degree of suffering, of course, vary from book to book,
but the theme of the joyless youngster is undeniably
pervasive. Marie-Claire Blais and Réjean Ducharme, it
should be admitted, are able to do this sort of thing
more imaginatively than many of the other writers, and
Ducharme skilfully tempers the morbid with humour
and poetic vision. But the vein of the tormented toddler
is surely wearing thin in the literary ores of French
Canada. Even Blais and Ducharme will not, I suspect, be
able to continue exploiting it without debilitating effect
upon their considerable artistic talents.

The second general observation about the child in
Canadian literature concerns fiction in both English and
French. As I mentioned earlier, the theme of innocence
as symbolized by a child is common in world literature.
Broadly speaking, children represent unspoiled purity
and dreams of a happy, perfect world. As they grow up
they become disillusioned—the purity is spoiled and the
dreams are shattered. The child then becomes the
symbol of a kind of paradise lost, celebrated inter-
nationally from the ancients through Jean-Jacques
Rousseau to John David Salinger. Upon reading
Canadian literature, however, one gets the impression
that the fictional child of this country is definitely not

representative of any kind of paradise, either possessed,
lost or to be sought. Apart from light works like Robert
Fontaine's *The Happy Time* and regional romances,
major Canadian novels do not even dwell upon the
innocence of childhood and subsequent disillusionment.
Whether because of the Calvinist-Jansenist insistence
upon original sin or the absence of positive national
myths, the typical child in Canadian literature seems to
be born disillusioned. If he has any dreams, they are
low-keyed and non-idealistic, like the desire for financial
security of Richler's Duddy Kravitz, Gabrielle Roy's
Jean Levesque and Florentine, or John Marlyn's Alex
Hunter. English-language writers are not so obsessed with
the tormented child as are their French-language counterparts, but certainly they tend to associate childhood with
unhappiness and anxiety. Suffice it to mention Leonard
Cohen's *The Favorite Game*, Ernest Buckler's *The
Mountain and the Valley*, John Marlyn's *Under the Ribs
of Death* and numerous episodes in the works of
Callaghan and MacLennan.

How significant this apparently distinctive tendency
of Canadian literature may be in terms of national
habits, parental behaviour, memory patterns and artistic
qualities, is difficult to say. It is, however, definitely
significant that the tendency should be shared by
writers of the different ethnic groups of Canada,
providing one more indication of the existence of a
common Canadian mystique.

The most striking common characteristic of Réjean
Ducharme's *L'Avalée des avalés* and W. O. Mitchell's
Who Has Seen the Wind is the extraordinary capacity
of each author to become totally immersed in the mind
and body of a child, or at least to convince the reader
that he has done so. Both novels have the ring of
authenticity, and both somehow escape the banality and
triteness one would expect to find coupled with this
authenticity, the very dangers which have discouraged

serious authors from adopting the technique of a child's point of view. Moreover, both Mitchell and Ducharme, in contrast to Marie-Claire Blais, Morley Callaghan and Leonard Cohen for instance, avoid using the child simply to explain the deficiencies, terrors or aberrations of the adult. Ducharme's Bérénice does reach physical maturity at the end of the book, but her mental state has not significantly changed—she is still a child emotionally. And of greatest importance with respect to engaging and holding the reader's interest, both Mitchell and Ducharme exhibit a gift for linguistic virtuosity and humour. It is undoubtedly this gift which sets *L'Avalée des avalés* and *Who Has Seen the Wind* above other books of the same species.

At first sight, the young protagonists of the two novels seem as different from each other as could possibly be imagined. Mitchell's Brian O'Connal is a relatively normal little boy in a relatively normal family, living in the ordinary way in a typical small town in the Canadian West. Bérénice Einberg of *L'Avalée des avalés* (which means, incidentally, "the girl who is the swallowed up of the swallowed up"—engulfing life and engulfed by life at the same time) is a precocious, disturbed child with a Polish Christian mother and a rich Jewish father who have reached the point of mutual hate, living in what is described as a converted abbey on an island near Montreal. By parental agreement, Bérénice is being brought up in the Jewish faith, while her brother Christian is following what his name implies. Bérénice is ignored by everyone, confused by opposing values and desperate for attention. Brian, on the other hand, is loved by reasonably well-adjusted parents and given plenty of attention at home and outside.

Upon closer examination, however, Brian and Bérénice are seen to be not so unlike one another. The difference between the two novels lies in the circumstances with which the children are confronted rather than in the children themselves. For instance, both Brian and Bérénice deeply resent the lack of attention which results from parents having other interests. In Brian's case, a baby brother quite naturally occupies his parents and grandmother at what he considers to be his expense. The situation becomes especially painful for Brian when the baby takes sick and needs undivided care. His grandmother, who has the job of keeping him out of the way, becomes the object of revenge fantasies:

> He hoped that Jake Harris brought his policeman knife and chopped her into little pieces and cut her head off for making him play outside . . . . He hated his grandmother. He hit the bump again, being careful that it was with the sharp edge and not the flat bottom of it. His grandmother had no colour in her hair, he thought, as he gripped the shovel more tightly and with both hands so that he could hit the sand with greater force. As the shovel rose and fell, he made thunder in the back of his throat; hot fire, he decided, was coming from his nose, and eyes, and ears and mouth. (pp. 4-5)

Now as one might expect, Brian soon gets over his resentment, for he is not really unloved and has only been temporarily neglected. His attention is quickly taken up by new discoveries, new games and different fantasies. For Bérénice, however, the circumstances are quite different. Her parents, estranged and preoccupied with their own emotional problems, do not in fact have any real love for her. Consequently, her revenge fantasies, much like Brian's to begin with, constantly become more elaborate as her resentment deepens into despair. Initially, she dwells upon her loneliness:

> You look all around, as if you're searching for something. You look, you look. You don't see

anything worthwhile. If you pay attention when you look around like that, you begin to see that what you're looking at hurts you, that you're alone and scared. There's nothing you can do about being alone and scared. Nothing helps. Hunger and thirst have their dandelions and rainwater. Fear and loneliness have nothing.[14]

In an attempt to escape isolation and solitude, or at least to make them more bearable, Bérénice more or less creates an imaginary world of her own, conditioned by her wide reading, and she invents her own playmate called Constance Chlore. But none of this can placate the resentment she feels, particularly against her mother. "Ma mère est un oiseau," she says. "Les oiseaux ne nous aiment pas. Aussitôt qu'ils nous voient, ils se sauvent." (p. 20) But then immediately after intimating that her mother is like a bird and does not love her, Bérénice modifies her view. She is afraid to state explicity what desperately she does not want to believe:

My mother is like a bird. When I put my arms around her, she goes stiff and pushes me away. Be quiet! Go play outside! You're hurting me! That's enough now! . . . . She loves me, but in a funny way. . . . When she was sitting among the flowers, I went over and sat on her and put my arms around her neck. Go and play like a good little girl. Leave mommy alone! Mommy is tired. When she was walking, I followed her, hanging on to her dress. She let me do it without paying any attention to me. Then she came back and told me that she had played with me enough.[15]

In *Who Has Seen the Wind* one finds adults, busy or preoccupied, shooing a child away in exactly the same way and with the same kind of language—"Get outside

96

now. Now be a good boy and do as ye're told. Just stay out of mother's way." But in Brian's case, the shooing away is balanced by equal amounts of genuine parental love. Bérénice does not experience any such balance. Some commentaries on *L'Avalée des avalés* have suggested that she can be explained as a child monster, abnormal, mentally deranged in some way. With this view I disagree. Bérénice, like Brian and any other normal child, wants only to love and to be loved. Repeatedly she expresses her desire for any sign of affection from her mother. "Je l'aime, je l'aime," she tells herself over and over again. When she takes sick, her desire for an indication of her mother's affection becomes more poignant than usual—"Je veux qu'elle se couche avec moi," she says. "Je ne sais comment le lui dire"—I don't know how to say it to her. Lack of response on the part of her mother, or on the part of anyone else for that matter, is what causes Bérénice to withdraw within herself, so that, pitifully, she is no longer able to communicate what she wants. Her resentment, like Brian's, is perfectly normal. But unlike Brian's, it is never assuaged, and it builds up beyond revenge fantasies to the point of desperation and action, which is also perfectly normal, however unfortunate in terms of human relations. One of these actions is to poison her mother's favourite cat, Mauriac. But the mother buys another cat and calls it Mauriac II. This time Bérénice gives full vent to the cruelty children can often display, a cruelty, incidentally, which Mitchell also describes, in a prairie scene where boys pull the tail off a live gopher. Bérénice traps Mauriac II and beats the animal to death with a club. Then she proceeds to enact an ancient revenge ritual—to be sure that her mother will suffer the maximum effect of losing her pet, she buries it with the stiffened tail sticking out of the ground.

Perhaps even more diabolical is Bérénice's triple

revenge on her mother, brother and cousin. She has often tried to find in her brother Christian the recognition she cannot get elsewhere. But here again, she receives no valid response. Christian has his own problems and interests. One of these interests is his beautiful cousin Mingrélie, apparently a Polish relative on the mother's side who comes to visit the Einbergs. Bérénice, who has developed an exaggerated image of her own ugliness, detests this girl on several counts. She naturally resents every moment that Christian and Mingrélie spend together, and she contrives to keep an eye on them at all times. Her big opportunity arrives when the young couple are innocently frolicking in a barn and the girl jabs herself on a pitchfork. Without thinking, Mingrélie removes her dress to avoid getting blood on it, whereupon the bashful Christian averts his eyes. The girl, however, cannot resist this little chance to test her equipment. "You can look if you like." she says. "It's not a crime. A Russian would look. I can't figure out Canadians at all. Look, Christian."[16] And not to be outdone by a Russian, Christian looks. Meanwhile, Bérénice has been spying and sees the opportunity to get three birds with one stone. She has long agonized in the knowledge that Christian is her mother's favourite, the son who can do no wrong. Rushing, she is able to bring her mother to the barn before Mingrélie, who is not exactly rushing, has gotten back into her dress.

The climactic stroke of Bérénice's programme of revenge on her mother and brother, to be sure, comes when she writes Christian a passionate love letter with strong undertones of incest, knowing full well that her father will read it. Given the antagonism between the father and mother, this letter results in Bérénice being shipped off to live with her father's relatives in New York. But it is too late. Emotionally, Bérénice is permanently crippled. She is incapable of a satisfactory relationship with anyone. An avid reader, she takes to pornography in large doses. Within the world of her imagination she plays with her own fantasies, having Constance Chlore killed in an automobile accident. Interestingly, she spends much time speculating on the nature of reality. If unreal people can be real in her mind, more real than real people, then in her mind she can control and dispose of anyone she wishes. After all, each of them exists only inasmuch as she is willing to admit his existence. She thus shuts herself increasingly in her own mental world. Nor can she find satisfaction in embracing a cause. At the end of the book she has become a girl soldier in the Arab-Israeli War. She has a hollow friendship with another girl, Gloria, but it ends sordidly when during an enemy attack Bérénice saves herself by forcefully holding Gloria in front of her to stop the bullets:

> Gloria was buried Tuesday. I got off with two arms in a sling. I lied to them. I told them that Gloria had thrown her body in front of me as a living shield. If you don't believe me, ask anyone what a pair of friends we were. They believed me. Of course, they needed a few heroines.[17]

Bérénice, then, finally completes her protective shell of egocentric cynicism, offering nothing to and expecting nothing from the outside world. She really has not changed a great deal from the child presented at the beginning of *L'Avalée des avalés*—she has simply plugged the holes in her armour. No more one-way emotional involvements. At the end of the book, as at the beginning, she says, "Je suis seule." (p. 8 and p. 266) Psychologically she is the understandable conditioned response to the circumstances of her life.

Exactly the same can be said about Brian in *Who Has Seen the Wind*. He too develops a cynical attitude, as a result of bitter experiences, including the early sudden death of his father, the death of his grandmother and his realization that the society around him contains a great measure of hypocrisy. It should be noted, however, that Brian does not go through stages of disillusionment. Because of the sober influence of his mother and father, and especially because of the earthy rowdiness and realism of his Uncle Sean, he has never built castles in the sky. Brian is simply shaped by his experiences. Like Bérénice, he eventually comes to ponder the meaning of reality. But unlike Bérénice, because he has experienced love and knows that goodness and justice can sometimes exist, however much they are thwarted by the Reverend Powellys and Mrs. Abercrombies, Brian does not reject the world around him. The meaning of life, like the wind, he is unable to grasp, but he is willing to continue the search:

> It had something to do with dying; it had something to do with being born. Loving something and being hungry were with it too. He knew that much now. There was the prairie; there was a meadow lark, a baby pigeon, and a colt with two heads. In some haunting way the Ben was part of it. So was Mr. Digby. (p. 343)

Thus the dénouement of *Who Has Seen the Wind* is quite different from that of *L'Avalée des avalés*. Yet however much these two books vary in detail, they both dramatize the same central theme, that the essential factor in moulding the nature of a child is love—love given and love received. Both books illustrate the fact that an emotional cripple—Bérénice, Muriel and Mrs. Abercrombie—is more pitiful and can be a greater danger to other people than can a mental or physical cripple. This theme, of course, is hardly new, although certainly Mitchell and Ducharme express it in ways which are engagingly original. Actually, as I suggested earlier, it is precisely in the areas of technique and style that these two authors achieve distinction. And it is in these areas that they have most in common.

The fascination which certain natural phenomena hold for a child and the delight of discovery are sensations captured and communicated convincingly by both Mitchell and Ducharme. Here, for example, is Brian noticing light reflected in dew drops:

> A twinkling of light caught his eye, and he turned his head to see that new flake leaves of the spirea were starred in the sunshine: on every leaf were drops that had gathered during the night. He got up. They lay limpid, cradled in the curve of the leaves, each with a dark lip of shadow under its curving side and a star's cold light in its pure heart. As he bent more closely over one, he saw the veins of the leaf blown up under the drop's perfect crystal curve. The barest breath of a wind stirred at his face, and its caress was part of the strange enchantment too. Within him something was opening, releasing shyly as the petals of a flower open, with such gradualness that he was hardly aware of it. But it was happening, an alchemy, imperceptible as the morning wind, a growing elation of such fleeting delicacy and poignancy that he dared not turn his mind to it for fear that he might spoil it, that it might be carried away as lightly as one strand of spider web on a sigh of a wind. (p. 125)

The following passage is Réjean Ducharme's description of Bérénice and Christian using a hemp cloth as a fisherman's net:

> Bent more and more over our little cloth, which is sinking with the weight of the water, we are more excited than if we were sifting gold. The water caught pours down between our legs, then begins to drip as

the cloth empties. Nothing is left now but a
thickening soup of silt and weeds. Then the muddy
water begins to move. It comes alive, starts to boil. I
try to make out what is emerging from this
unbearable gestation, imagining I don't know what
kind of wriggling ear-rings, miniscule finned fairies,
living flowers like daisies and dahlias. The ferment
becomes more defined, becomes populated. Tiny
backs glitter. Tails become visible. Already I can see a
mass of little black tadpoles stirring. I am waiting to
see more, the big ones, pale and tepid like a sparrow's
eggs, with throats white and soft like a cheek, the big
ones that are growing stick legs at the base of
beautiful tails like lance tips crumbling away. Beside
the others they are giants, marvellous, almost
monstrous. They fill your hand when you squeeze to
feel life working in them. Every time, when the water
has all emptied out, a kind of miracle happens. A
leech as big as a shoe-lace leaps up, quivering from
end to end. A real little aquarium fish, a little
transparent fish glittering green or blue breaking away
from the mass of small black tadpoles and tiny
shells.[18]

Throughout *Who Has Seen the Wind* and *L'Avalée des
avalés* one finds similar detail and imagery, the type of
detail one feels a child would notice and the type of
image—sparrow's eggs, a strand of spider web—one can
accept that a child might conceive. The pure effect of
beauty, on a youngster who does not yet know what
beauty is supposed to be, who does not understand why
a new sensation is being created within him, but who
knows that he wants to hold on to it—all this is
effectively communicated in Mitchell's passage, causing
the reader perhaps to wonder what sophisticated taste
and art appreciation really signify. The child's wonder at
life itself, holding the tadpole in her hand and feeling

that it is alive, is transmitted to the reader by Ducharme.

The two authors, moreover, explore a wide range of reactions, from that caused by the commonplace such as in the passages above to the bewilderment occasioned by the bizarre, such as the two-headed calf which Brian sees or the huge rat which Bérénice witnesses chewing off its own leg to escape a trap. As might be expected, Brian being less wrapped up in himself is more aware of external phenomena than is Bérénice, who spends more time dissecting her own feelings and anxieties. In communicating this interior exploration, Ducharme uses a greater amount of poetic imagery than can be found in Mitchell's writing. Comparing herself to the cousin she envies, Bérénice says, "Je suis hideuse. Mes cheveux sont si raides et si enchevêtrés qu'un peigne bulldozer y tomberait en panne. Mingrélie est belle comme un jour sans fin." (p. 43)—I am hideous. My hair is so coarse and tangled that it would wreck a bulldozer comb. Mingrélie is beautiful like a day without end. In *L'Avalée des avalés* there are patterns of imagery, such as the comparison of Bérénice's mother to a bird, one instance of which was noted earlier. Birds are beautiful, but cold and distant, and they fly away as soon as a person tries to approach. When Bérénice is sick and desperate for affection she thinks especially of a hummingbird, the extreme of beauty and timidity. She is afraid to become too demonstrative lest her mother "va s'envoler comme un oiseau-mouche qui entend remuer dans les branches." (p. 108)

The difficulty that a child often has to apprehend traditional concepts of God is examined at length by both W. O. Mitchell and Réjean Ducharme. In *Who Has Seen the Wind* the potential for humour is exploited to the full when Brian, having observed that people of consequence are referred to by their initials and occasionally have letters following their names, comes up with "R. W. God, B.V.D.," who rides the sky on a vacuum cleaner. Equally childlike but more pregnant with irony is Brian's comment, after he has been given the orthodox assurance that God controls everything—"God isn't very considerate—is He, Gramma?" Bérénice also has trouble reconciling the God of Love with the "Dieu des Armées"—the French expression which seems to have a far stronger impact than the quaint English equivalent "Lord of Hosts." As noted earlier, Bérénice is being brought up in the Jewish faith. Here is her reaction to a synagogue service:

Rabbi Schneider talks about people who don't fear the true God. He says that the Lord of Hosts has stated that he will strike down with lightning anybody who doesn't fear Him, that He will leave them with neither root nor leaf. If Rabbi Schneider thinks that I'm afraid, he's barking up the wrong tree. The shivers He gives me, his "Lord of Hosts," are shivers of anger. The more he talks about it, the more I despise Him. They have a God just like themselves, in their own image and shape, a God who can't restrain himself from hating, a God who grinds his teeth, his pangs of hate are so strong. When Rabbi Schneider speaks like that, I think of my elm tree. My elm tree stands in the middle of our big island, alone like an airplane in the sky. It must be a sinner. I've never seen it with leaves. Its bark falls to pieces; you can tear it up like paper. Under the bark it is smooth smooth, soft soft. When the wind blows and its great dry branches crackle, you would say it was full of skeletons.[19]

Bérénice, of course, is more bitter about the way God has supposedly ordered the world than is Brian. Also, she has grown up with opposing religious beliefs constantly being paraded before her; consequently, it is understandable that she should become more sceptical more rapidly than her counterpart in *Who Has Seen the Wind*.

By now, possibly, I have presented enough quotations and translations to give some hint of the linguistic virtuosity which characterizes the work of both W. O. Mitchell and Réjean Ducharme. The latter must perforce lose a great deal in translation, for the effect of his writing sometimes depends equally upon sound and meaning. Lines like the following for example—"Je dis n'importe quoi. Ma robe! Ma brobe! Ma crobe! Ma frobe! Ma trobe! Ma vrobe!" (p. 87) cannot be done full justice in translation, needless to say. Or: "Ici, il fait mauvais! Ici, il fait décadacrouticaltaque!" (p. 130) Ducharme takes delight in repeating the vowels and suffixes of the French language: "Le plus important est que Chamoror ou Einberg les lisent, soient scandalisés, découragés, abasourdis, écoeurés (p. 144). . . . Ce n'est pas fascinant, c'est avalant, étouffant, asphyxiant (p. 150) . . . . Qui n'est pas avalé, militairement, administrativement, judiciairement, monétairement et religieusement?" (p. 160) He often uses puns and plays on words—the name Mordecai becomes "Morde-à-Caille," phooey becomes "Fouï." And what does the translator into English do with *"Baby you're so square*! (chanson populaire). Bébé tu es tellement carée!" (p. 171)?

Actually, it is Ducharme's obvious fascination with sounds and words which in turn fascinates the reader. Since his whole book is a monologue—spoken language —he provides himself with the maximum opportunity to exploit linguistic possibilities. But such opportunity is not without pitfalls. Choosing as his protagonist a precocious, sensitive little girl who fights solitude by reading, listening, talking to herself and amusing herself with language games, he avoids the tedium which some people feel halfway through Salinger's *Catcher in the*

Rye, after reading the same teenage cliché for the fiftieth time. When Bérénice repeats herself, the reader, like the audience for whom the Homeric epithet was devised, is happy to be able momentarily to lower his alertness level.

As for W. O. Mitchell in *Who Has Seen the Wind*, he also achieves linguistic virtuosity through representation of the spoken language. The crude and colourful diction of Uncle Sean, as close to the soil as the man himself, for example: "Goddam their souls as green and hard as God's little green apples! Goddam their goddam souls." (p. 70) Mitchell's high point, to my mind, is reached in the monologues—amazing concoctions of Biblical phrases, rural dialect and evangelical rhetoric—of the religious nut Saint Sammy, expounding on his collection of underwear labels or giving his version of the Book of Genesis. The following passage, describing the storm which Saint Sammy considers God has sent for his benefit, is a rare piece of stylistic skill:

Sammy, Sammy, this is her, and I say ontuh you she is a dandy! Moreover I have tried her out! I have blew over Tourigny's henhouse; I have uprooted Dan Tate's windbreak, tooken the back door off of the schoolhouse, turned over the girls' toilet, three racks, six grain wagons; I have blew down the power line in four places; I have wrecked the sails on Magnus Petersen's windmill! In two hours did I cook her up; in two hours will I cook her down! An' when she hath died down, go you ontuh Bent Candy's where he languishes an' you shall hear the gnashing of teeth which are Bent Candy's an' he shall be confounded! Thus seth the Lord God of Hosts, enter intuh thy pianah box an' hide fer the fear a the Lord! Take the Kid with you! (pp. 308-9)

There is no mystery, then, about the reasons for the

effectiveness and excellence of both Mitchell's *Who Has Seen the Wind* and Ducharme's *L'Avalée des avalés*. If the latter, with its detailed portrait of intense and soul-destroying deprivation, can be described as powerful, then Mitchell's book, with its landscape of human feeling in so many of its subtle shades and forms, can only be described as beautiful. There is also no question about the thematic and technical qualities these two books have in common.

To return to the observations made at the beginning of this essay, however, one still wonders why Canadian literature should have the possibly unique distinction of two such books successfully exploiting the point of view of a child. Moreover, why should both children, like so many other children in Canadian fiction, be presented as relatively non-idealistic, even cynical?

There is one plausible explanation. Canada, as we know, has been conditioned by the Puritan ethos, Jansenist in Québec and Calvinist elsewhere, as the essay preceding this one explains. Can it be that this influence has resulted in children having a premature sense of sin, or at least in adults remembering this sense of sin more vividly than they recall the carefree joys of childhood? The Puritan ethos, of course, has always stressed the evil of carefree joy, even in children. One of the most startling passages in the writings of the great Puritan preacher Jonathan Edwards is his triumphant description of how he made a small child aware of the wickedness in his soul! How demons and devils and various religion-spawned bogeymen were used to make youngsters "be good" in French Canada is related by numerous writers, including Louis Hémon in *Maria Chapdelaine*. And interestingly enough, although *Who Has Seen the Wind* and *L'Avalée des avalés* concern two different periods in the history of Canada, the thirties and the sixties, both books dwell upon the effect that a thoroughly inculcated sense of guilt can have on a young mind. Mitchell tells of Brian's traumatic experience after his teacher pronounces that the "Lord punishes little boys who don't wash their hands and then say that they did." (p. 107) In Ducharme's book it is Christian who suffers similar anguish for a similarly ridiculous reason, in his case innocent liberties with his kissing-cousin Mingrélie. "Je suis damné! Je suis damné!" he confesses to Bérénice. "Personne ne peut plus rien pour moi." (p. 122) Clearly, therefore, both Mitchell and Ducharme feel that a premature and distorted sense of guilt is still an important part of the experience of the child in twentieth-century Canada.

But the winds are changing. The Old Order of traditional values has now largely disappeared. Brian and Bérénice themselves, living in rapidly evolving societies, are children of changing winds. With the increasing number of broken marriages and inter-cultural contacts, Ducharme's Bérénice may possibly be more repre-sentative of the contemporary scene than is Mitchell's Brian. On the other hand, there must still be many Brians, reasonably secure in their emotions, doing more or less what they are expected to do in life and groping for the meaning of it all, trying to see the wind. And they, like the characters created by W. O. Mitchell and Réjean Ducharme, will discover that they are not able to see it. Like Brian and Bérénice, they will simply be aware from time to time that the wind is passing by.

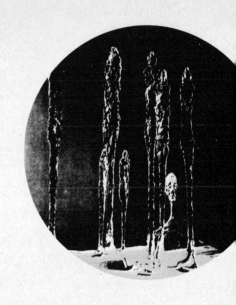

The Fourth Kind of Separatism

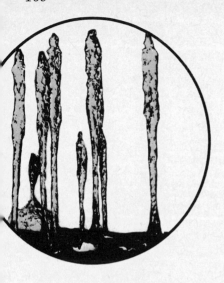

There are four kinds of Separatism in the province of
Québec. The first kind, manifested in mailbox bombings
and other acts of noisy desperation, forms the subject
matter of Hubert Aquin's *Prochain épisode*, Claude
Jasmin's *Ethel et le terroriste*, Ellis Portal's *Killing
Ground*, Pierre Gravel's *A Perte de temps*, and to some
extent of Jacques Godbout's *Le Couteau sur la table*,
James Bacque's *The Lonely Ones* and Hugh MacLennan's
Return of the Sphinx. Based upon the fairly reliable
premise that an established power structure will never
voluntarily relinquish power, it is an attitude which is
hardly new to the world or to Québec. It is, for
instance, the theme of a minor French-Canadian novel
published nearly thirty years ago—Rex Desmarchais's *La
Chesnaie*. Despite a hero modelled after the Portuguese
dictator Antonio Salazar and a revolution somehow
intended to take up where Papineau left off in 1841,
Desmarchais's novel did not create much of a stir.

Recently, however, there have been a number of stirs, and a great deal of writing in addition to the novels listed above. The first kind of Separatism, then, whatever menace it may represent for the Canadian nation, has certainly been a shot in the arm for Canadian literature.

The second kind of Separatism in Québec is illustrated by René Lévesque and his Parti Québécois, although there is some doubt as to how wholeheartedly all the members of the party share Lévesque's articulate moderation. He is, of course, just as dedicated to the goal of an autonomous state of Québec as are the adherents of the first brand of Separatism. The distinguishing feature of his attitude is that he has repeatedly rejected violence and force. Like the Scottish nationalists, he feels that independence must be achieved by means of the electoral system. As soon as the Parti Québécois elects a majority of representatives to the Provincial Government, there will no longer be a provincial government.

Another distinguishing feature of Lévesque's philosophy is that a future separate Québec would maintain economic union with the rest of Canada, thus possibly avoiding the often-suggested danger of becoming a hockey-stick and maple-sugar republic. René Lévesque justifies his position by the argument that only national independence can cure the frustrations and inferiority complex which have long haunted French Canada. Only independence can restore group pride and self-confidence. A benevolent federalism, like a loving mother who will not or cannot untie the apron strings, can never fulfil the psychological needs of a people who have come of age. And just as a grown girl does not want her mother to choose her boyfriends, Québec wishes to conduct her own external affairs.

René Lévesque, to be sure, did not invent the second kind of Separatism. Actually the idea, in somewhat primitive form perhaps, was used in fiction long before even Rex Desmarchais's *La Chesnaie*. The novel *Pour la patrie* by Jules-Paul Tardivel, which appeared in 1895, projects a sovereign Québec achieved constitutionally despite the intrigues of federal ministers and a full-scale, John-Birch-Society-style Freemason plot. As a prophet the fanaticism-prone Tardivel was a bit of a flop, for he predicted the establishment of "La République de Nouvelle France" in 1945. From the point of view of language learning, however, he ought to be an inspiration to many English-speaking Canadians, for when this man who was to become a journalist for *Le Canadien* and write several volumes of prose, came at the age of seventeen to Saint-Hyacinthe from his birthplace of Covington, Kentucky, he could not speak French!

I might note here, incidentally, that a significant difference between the old-style Separatism of people like Tardivel and Lionel Groulx and the new Separatism of René Lévesque is that Lévesque envisages a progressive, modern state. Ironically, the nationalistic extremists of yesteryear were essentially reactionary rather than revolutionary. They wanted to recapture a part of the past, to preserve religion and the old traditions, to return to the womb of the Holy Mother and the garden of agrarian purity (Québec's climate somewhat cramping the notion of paradise). Lévesque's Separatism, it must be said, does not seek to recapture anything of the past, but to pour the future into new moulds.

The other two kinds of Separatism have not been so widely publicized as the first two. There is the Separatism of those who do not really want a politically independent Québec, but who have learned that the Separatist Movement can be a useful lever to obtain concessions from English Canada, and even from the United States and France. Whereas the other brands of Separatism are nourished by the fears in the hearts of

French Canadians, this kind reverses the situation and exploits the fears and aspirations of those who are not French Canadians. Once again, the principle is time-honoured and productive—it has long been used by politicians in the American South and more recently by the "block-busters" in the American North.

The fourth variety of Separatism is the opposite of the third, and it is undoubtedly the most significant of all four. It is the genuine desire for group self-determination which is shared by thousands, perhaps millions of French Canadians who nevertheless refuse to declare themselves Separatists. These people are the confused masses. They know there is something wrong. They feel frustrated and dehumanized, manipulated by a system which they vaguely identify with English Canada and the United States. But because the identification is vague, and because the positive stance of the terrorist groups seems an over-simplification; because the terrorism itself is alien to their thinking, and apparently futile; because these people have been conditioned over the centuries to accept the imperfections of life on earth, they have not as yet openly committed themselves. Many are afraid to do so; others do not know how. At the moment they are Separatists inasmuch as they wish to protect themselves, build a wall around themselves, escape from something, escape from the boiling ocean of North American society and gain the reassuring warmth of the family circle. As I have said, these people vaguely identify the oppression they feel with English Canada and the United States, often grouping the two together under the term *mentalité anglo-saxonne*. If ever Québec actually does secede from the Canadian union, it will be because this vague identification has been changed to something positive and specific. And not necessarily with benefit of logic.

The four kinds of Québec Separatism, then—terrorist, political, opportunist and psychological—are quite distinct from one another, and it seems to me that a knowledge of these distinguishing characteristics is a necessary prelude to examination of the literature of Separatism. Hubert Aquin's *Prochain épisode*, for example, was written by a man who at one time openly embraced the attitudes of our first category: the book was supposedly composed while Aquin was being detained in a Montreal jail after his arrest for alleged terrorist activities. It is an unusual, highly original novel, inter-weaving an *apologia pro vita sua* with a spy story and using both threads to present symbolic and direct commentaries on the malaise of Québec.

This malaise is eloquently sung from the beginning to the end of the book. It is tied up with the narrator's personal frustration. "Le salaire du guerrier défait," says Aquin, "c'est la dépression. Le salaire de la dépression nationale, c'est mon échec." (p. 26) A little later he comments: "C'est vrai que nous n'avons pas d'histoire. Nous n'aurons d'histoire qu'à partir du moment incertain où commencera la guerre révolutionnaire. Notre histoire s'inaugurera dans le sang d'une révolution qui me brise et que j'ai mal servie; ce jour-là, veines ouvertes, nous ferons nos débuts dans le monde." (p. 94) Here as in Negro America, violence is regarded as a necessary ritual—the new identity must be baptized in blood and in fire: "Un sacrement apocryphe nous lie indissolublement à la révolution. Ce que nous avons commencé, nous le finirons." (p. 74)

But the novel has another aspect. Interwoven with the narrator's agonized protestations is a description of the events which make up the first episode, or at least the episode which precedes what is to be *le prochain épisode*. This story is an intriguing allegory. H. de Heutz in his several guises of historian, financier and govern-ment agent is a symbol of English Canada and the Canadian power stucture, or the Establishment if you will. K., the girl with the long blond hair whom the narrator loves passionately and who is presumably his inspiration and accomplice in the attempt to eliminate H. de Heutz, is symbolic of *Québec* and the *Québecois.* In the usual spy-thriller way, the narrator follows the trail left by H. de Heutz, becoming more and more fascinated as he picks up additional bits of information about his many-sided quarry. The true identity of H. de Heutz becomes increasingly cloudy. He has other names and personalities. And he is cunningly dangerous. When the narrator eventually finds him in Geneva, he is himself overpowered and becomes a prisoner. Taken to H. de Heutz's chateau for questioning, the narrator invents a classic sob-story about abandoning his wife and two children because of debts and then lacking the courage to rob a bank or kill himself with the gun found on his person. H. de Heutz, of course, dismisses the story, but the narrator manages to catch him off-guard, grabs the revolver, and the tables are turned.

Then the plot takes a curious twist. When the narrator has transported H. de Heutz to a forest and is about to shoot him, the latter begins to weep pitifully and plead for his life. Then to the narrator's mystification, he repeats exactly the same sob-story that the narrator had used shortly before. This incredible development has a hypnotic effect on the narrator. He hesitates. And before he can condition himself to perform the execution, a friend of H. de Heutz has crept up behind him and the intended victim escapes. The friend, incidentally, is a girl with long blond hair.

The narrator has one more unsuccessful encounter with H. de Heutz, then he is instructed to return to Montreal, where plainclothes policemen, one of whom is hidden in a confessional booth, capture him in the Nôtre Dame Church.

What does all this mean? For one thing, Aquin appears to be saying that the narrator, the would-be terrorist executioner, fails because H. de Heutz, despite his chateau with a reproduction of Benjamin West's "The Death of General Wolfe" hanging on the wall, does not correspond to the narrator's idea of what his antagonist ought to be. And the correspondence becomes less and less satisfactory the more the narrator finds out about H. de Heutz. Toward the end of the novel he says: "H. de Heutz ne m'a jamais paru aussie mystérieux qu'en ce moment même, dans ce château qu'il hante élégamment. Mais l'homme que j'attends est-il bien l'agent ennemi que je dois faire disparaître froidement. Cela me paraît incroyable, car l'homme qui demeure ici transcende avec éclat l'image que je me suis faite de ma victime." (p. 129)

Moreover, the narrator and H. de Heutz are strangely alike in many respects. They share a taste for history and historical objects. Their identical sob-stories indicate emotional interinvolvement and similar patterns of thought. At one point, the narrator even mentions that he feels he is almost a spiritual medium for H. de Heutz. In short, the narrator fails because he cannot really identify his intended victim with an enemy who must be destroyed. He has developed a Hamlet complex. He is like a boxer who, confronted with a certain opponent, is unable to muster enough killer instinct.

There is also the suggestion—more than a suggestion really, for why else would Aquin repeatedly include the detail—that H. de Heutz's blond girl friend is actually the narrator's beloved K., who has been up to a little double-dealing. Aquin's terrorist group, as we know, was not supported by the populace of Québec. In fact, the ring was broken by Québec police. And the capture of the novel's protagonist in a church is probably Aquin's way of saying that *la résignation chrétienne* which has long been preached in Québec, is not the stuff to light the fires of revolution.

Some critics, understandably enough, have regarded *Prochain épisode* as a sort of manifesto for the first of

the four brands of Separatism defined at the beginning
of this analysis. Certainly it deals with terrorist ideas and,
as we have seen, in certain moods the narrator calls for
blood and revolution. On close examination, however,
the novel is unmistakably a negation of terrorism, a
striking dramatization of the futility of violent intervention. "Je suis devenue ce révolutionnaire voué à la
tristesse et à l'inutile éclatement de sa rage d'enfant,"
says the narrator toward the end of the book. (p. 137)
What *Prochain épisode* does provide is an expression,
and a convincing expression indeed, of the desperate
frustrations which have resulted in our fourth kind of
Separatism, the Separatism of the confused masses.
"C'est terrible et je ne peux plus me le cacher: je suis
désespéré," writes Aquin. "On ne m'avait pas dit qu'en
devenant patriote, je serais jeté ainsi dans la détresse et
qu'à force de vouloir la liberté, je me retrouverais
enfermé." (p. 27) The idea that to struggle for
something better might well lead to something worse is
undoubtedly one of the reasons why neither the
terrorist front nor René Lévesque has yet been able to
conscript the masses of French Canadians. Nevertheless,
the malaise—the fear of being swallowed up and having
all identity destroyed by the amorphous monster of
North American society—remains undiminished: "J'ai
peur de me réveiller dégénéré, complètement
désidentifié, anéanti. Un autre que moi, les yeux hagards
et le cerveau purgé de toute antériorité, franchira la
grille le jour de ma libération." (p. 47) The narrator goes
on to say that he does not know what the *prochain
épisode* will be. But he does know that something has
got to give, and I have no doubt that he speaks for
millions more than himself when he says, "je porte en
moi le germe de la révolution." (p. 171)

There are a number of parallels between Aquin's
book and Claude Jasmin's *Ethel et le terroriste*. Both
novels derive from the F.L.Q. activities which led to the

death of an elderly watchman in a bomb blast behind an
Army recruiting center on Montreal's Sherbrooke
Street. Jasmin, however, takes an objective approach,
analysing the psychology of a young man who plants
such a bomb and then goes to New York in an attempt
to escape. Paul, the young man, becomes a terrorist
partly because of the same sense of personal and group
frustration which haunts the narrator of *Prochain
épisode.* His reminiscence of Québec vividly reveals this
feeling:

> My country served up like rotten meat more than a
> hundred years ago to a band of long-toothed loyalists.
> My country stuffed with multicoloured cassocks,
> small-time grocers, skinny woodcutters, a few isolated
> giants, exceptions providing the material for our
> legends, which a great joker with a beaver face sings
> at the top of his voice to our pimply college boys, to
> our decrepit functionaries, to our street-corner
> clerks—in Parliament we have nothing but a bunch of
> fat-arsed whore-mongers with their noses buried in
> huge cheeses made of taxes, taxes collected from the
> two-bit grocers and functionaries, nothing but an
> army of gnawing rodents who have themselves blessed
> every Sunday, who parade about spouting stupidities
> which are taken for promises. They get themselves
> elected with no bother at all by fooling the people,
> by muddling the wits of our grocer-functionaries.
> And in the wings of this theatre of vermin, the
> cassocks and the loyalists clap their hands.[20]

Québec, curiously like Nova Scotia with its exiled
Highlanders and dark clouds of religion, has nurtured
its legends of giants to offset the nothingness in the lives
of ordinary men. Paul, in Jasmin's *Ethel et le terroriste,*
must have more than legends for sustenance. The author
shows how the terrorist organization provides for him,

as it does for other members, a chance to do something significant for the first time, a chance to fill a void which the conditions of life in Québec and in Canada have not been able to fill. Speaking of his reception in the organization, Paul says, "Et on m'a serré les mains. On m'a dit que j'étais indispensable! Tu entends. On ne m'a jamais dit ça, sais-tu." (p. 46) On another occasion he says,"Je ne suis plus un simple 'canoque' de quartier du parc Lafontaine. Des héros." (p. 21) And when the time comes for Paul to do his part, he acts blindly, unthinkingly: "J'en ai des tics pour un long moment, et puis après? J'avais des ordres. Oui. C'est ce que je voulais. A un moment, j'ai fait ni un ni deux, j'ai dit aux gars: 'donnez-moi le paquet, l'heure, l'endroit.' C'est tout. Je ne voulais rien savoir. J'avais besoin d'un travail aveugle." (p. 17) And like many of the desperate men who jump from bridges or hijack airliners, Paul has his brief moment in the sun.

Jasmin's story, however, goes beyond the simple delineation of a character unbalanced by a need for recognition. The book suggests that many of the other members of the terrorist organization fit into that category, with various added personal neuroses to spur their hate; and so far as the typical terrorist is concerned, Jasmin is probably not far from the truth. But Paul, like the narrator of *Prochain épisode*, has enemy-identification problems. He finds it easier to love than to hate. In particular, he passionately loves Ethel, who is Jewish. Ethel shares his feelings of frustration. She shares his moments of childlike joy, his essential innocence. She can even share his aspirations and understand his need for release through violence. But she cannot endorse group hatred and murder, and naturally the terrorist group is dependent on group hatred. Paul is told that he must abandon Ethel, something which he cannot and will not do. Thus he ends up in an impossible situation, alienated from his former gang members and being propositioned by the police to save himself by turning stool pigeon. His only sympathizer besides Ethel is an American Negro professor called Slide, who has been collaborating with the terrorist group, but who has become disillusioned by the group's drift from "Third-World" idealism to gutter xenophobia. Paul, then, like the protagonist of *Prochain épisode*, is a failure as a terrorist.

Also a failure is the protagonist of Pierre Gravel's *A Perte de temps*, another novel which analyses the psychology of terrorism. Gravel's treatment of the subject is much the same as Jasmin's, although less dramatic. The climax of *A Perte de temps* comes when Robert's sweetheart, Marie, suggests that the two escape to Mexico. Unlike Jasmin's Paul, Robert cannot leave. "Partir, ce serait renier, abandonner, couper soi-même les ponts qu'on avait érigés," he reasons logically (p. 89), underlining the crucial difference between ordinary crime and terrorist activity based upon philosophical convictions. But the activity is also based upon personal frustration and despair. Son of a father who had quietly killed himself one day, Robert simply walks into the arms of the police.

But while Pierre Gravel, Claude Jasmin and Hubert Aquin dramatize the futility of terrorism, they nevertheless confirm the existence of an explosive malaise in Québec. Jasmin does not see it as something limited to Québec. He sees Québec's problem as part of a fairly universal unrest, which of course it is. Toward the end of the novel, Paul tells Ethel:

The campaign that must be fought. You know, the war, the true war. The struggle to throw off this great fat cow, this diseased and lazy animal that is lying on top of us all. On your country and on mine. On the black people, on the people of Greece, on those of Turkey and on those of China and Scotland. An

enormous beast. The evil, Ethel, the true evil, the
only one—it's ignorance. That is what should be
fought. That is the true enemy. Our only enemy.
Ignorance. Nothing, Ethel, is more serious or worse
than ignorance. That is what seeds confusion, what
fosters mediocrity, taboos and prejudices.[21]

Jasmin thus identifies the desperation currently
manifest in Québec as essentially part of a world-wide
phenomenon. He is, of course, not alone in making such
an observation. Other Québec writers, including Aquin,
have said much the same thing, as does James Bacque in
his novel *The Lonely Ones.* The term *nègre blanc* has
come into use (notably, but not exclusively in Pierre
Vallières' *Nègres blancs de l'Amérique*), and its legitimacy with respect to French Canadians was recently the
subject of a lengthy analysis of Max Dorsinville.[22] Such
books as Jacques Renaud's *Le Cassé* or Roch Carrier's
La Guerre, yes sir! convey a sense of depression and
hopelessness subject to momentary eruption in violence,
as a condition of life hardly peculiar to the province of
Québec. Jacques Godbout's *Le Couteau sur la table* is
even more explicit.

It is a cunning book, packed with subtle undertones
and connotations. As in the novels of Aquin and Jasmin,
the deep involvement of the protagonist with a girl has
particular symbolic meaning. Godbout's Patricia—rich,
blond, beautiful, the ultimate in female comfort and
accommodation—represents the affluent North
American society, the land of the Lotus Eaters from
which the protagonist cannot easily withdraw. She is
the jet set, gourmet food, flashy motels and Florida
vacations. When he speaks to her of the struggles of
oppressed peoples, of the threat of nuclear bombs, or of
his own bitter existential vacuum, she responds by
offering him her splendid body, showered and per-
fumed. Then, being half-Jewish and half-Irish in origin,

Patricia combines two ethnic traditions which have long
had special significance in French Canada. Each of the
two groups has had a love-hate relationship with *les
Québécois*. It has been possible to identify with the
Jews as a cultural-religious entity surviving against great
odds, and with the Irish as Roman Catholic Celts
victimized by English oppression. On the other side of
the .coin, French Canadians have thought themselves
exploited by Jewish businessmen and endangered by the
assimilation potential of their English-speaking, *vendus*
Irish coreligionists. It is, therefore, understandable that
Godbout's protagonist should have a love-hate relationship with Patricia.

At the end of the book he acquires another girl
friend, Madeleine, who symbolizes French Canada, the
quiet, obedient French Canada of days gone by. But he
does not give up Patricia. Indeed, the three of them live
together in an apartment on Mountain Street in
Montreal, with Madeleine temporarily occupying the
hero's emotional energy and Patricia his prime-time
Sunday afternoons. Shortly, however, Madeleine is
killed in an accident—decapitated by a truck while riding
the narrator's motorcycle. A funeral parlour scene
symbolizes the death of Québec's old order, which the
protagonist can witness with interest but without
particular regret. Then he proceeds to seduce
Madeleine's little sister Monique.

Throughout *Le Couteau sur la table* Godbout makes
recurrent reference to nursery rimes. Such rimes, of
course, are the most basic and simple indicators of
cultural differences. Moreover, the rime "I, ni, mi, ni,
maï, ni, mo," which turns up most often, signifies the
state of indecision in the narrator's mind. As the story
ends, despite the stirrings aroused by Madeleine, her
sister and the Separatist Movement, the protagonist
remains in a state of indecision. Patricia is still there.
But his attitude toward her has changed. "Je ne te ferai

aucun mal, si tu ne dis mot, Patricia," he says. "D'ailleurs il ne te servirait à rien de te débattre ou de crier, ou même de parler de nos amours anciennes. Le couteau restera sur la table de la cuisine." (pp. 157-8) The knife is on the table.

In essence, therefore, all of these French-Canadian novels dramatize our fourth kind of Separatism. All of them emphasize the pressing desire for action and the potential for violence. As the announcement on the back cover of Jasmin's *Ethel et le terroriste* puts it: "Tout jeune Québécois de vingt ans porte théoriquement une bombe sous le bras." The factor which prevents the theory from becoming practice and wholesale support of Separatism is the difficulty of isolating and identifying the enemy. English Canada and federalism have been readily pinpointed by some, but have not as yet been accepted as the malignant tumour by the many.

Moreover, as James Bacque's *The Lonely Ones* dramatically illustrates, the old notion of Canada's primary tension being between anglophone and francophone, between English-Canadian establishment and French-Canadian worker, is becoming further and further removed from the whole truth and the complex reality. Bacque's novel, of course, was not intended as a socio-philosophical analysis of Separatism or of terrorism, but rather as a psychological study of two individuals, Harry Summers and André Riancourt. From the book, however, significant implications emerge. Harry and André, products of the two different cultural traditions of Canada, are both artists. But they discover that when crisis occurs, they have more in common than profession, more in fact than either might have admitted or suspected. At the end of the book, both men become inadvertently involved in a terrorist murder, and Harry turns out to be André's most reliable friend. The crisis, ironically, while it italicizes each man's individuality, does not divide them but binds them more closely together. What these two Canadian characters have in common is stronger and more fundamental that what they do not share. Which, interestingly enough, is precisely the conclusion we have come to regarding the two literary traditions of Canada.

Of the two English-Canadian novels which focus on Separatism itself, Hugh MacLennan's *Return of the Sphinx* and Ellis Portal's *Killing Ground*, the second need not occupy much of our time. Portal's novel is not an attempt to analyse motivations or to offer insight into sociological and psychological realities. Rather it is a projection of what would happen to Canada if ever civil war were to become a fact. As such, it makes a point. Canadians are just as capable of bestiality and cold-blooded slaughter as any other civilized Christian nation. Naturally there would be a mess. Portal's novel, however, is marred by overabundance of sensational detail, which reinforces rather than suspends the reader's disbelief. Raping the enemy's beautiful women is a common human response hallowed by tradition; chopping off their breasts with Bren gun blasts is a little too bizarre. The book eventually deteriorates into a comic-opera sequence of events, including wife-stealing and interchange of roles.

Hugh MacLennan's *Return of the Sphinx*, on the other hand, contains a great many insights which are pertinent and valuable. Toronto book reviewers and the Governor-General's Award committee notwithstanding, it is probably the most important Canadian novel to appear for many years. I emphasize the word Canadian, and I am going to make a general observation about the works of Hugh MacLennan which may disturb some critics in this country. As I have become more and more deeply involved and conversant with Canadian literature in both languages, it has become increasingly evident to me that Hugh MacLennan is one of the few writers in the emerging mainstream of Canadian literature. By mainstream I mean that sphere of experience, consciousness and identification which is essentially and peculiarly Canadian. Every writer must perforce operate within a particular emotional and intellectual sphere of consciousness, and among Canadian writers several such spheres can be discerned. With few exceptions, these spheres of consciousness are defined and restricted by geographical area—rural Ontario, the small town, the prairies, the Atlantic seaboard, rural Québec, Québec City, English Montreal, French Montreal, Toronto, Vancouver, Winnipeg. Furthermore, for English-Canadian writers the broader spheres of consciousness are ones which have been defined by American writers, or at least are shared with them. The small town of Sherwood Anderson, for instance, is much the same as the small town of Sinclair Ross or W. O. Mitchell. The border does not really exist for the prairie sphere of consciousness. Stephen Leacock made a point of leaving his readers free to imagine that his settings could be almost anywhere in North America.

What, then, is a sphere of consciousness essentially and peculiarly Canadian? I should think that the main distinguishing feature would have to be dependent upon the main distinguishing feature of the Canadian nation —the coexistence of two major ethnic groups. To be in the emerging mainstream of Canadian literature, therefore, a writer must have some awareness of fundamental aspects and attitudes of both language groups in Canada.

It is just such awareness on the part of a few which is slowly moulding a single, common Canadian mystique out of the previous parallel threads of evolution. The parallel threads, of course, are still there, and the majority of Canadian writers seem content, in some cases consciously determined, to continue the process. But Hugh MacLennan is one exception. And not only is MacLennan one of the few in the mainstream; his body of works is the current which has given that mainstream definition and momentum. It is not surprising that the perceptive American critic Edmund Wilson, in describing his reaction to Hugh MacLennan, should say "I came to recognize that there did not exist a Canadian way of looking at things." Nor is it without significance that George Woodcock should entitle his classic essay on MacLennan "A Nation's Odyssey." So many other Canadian writers—good writers such as Sinclair Ross, Morley Callaghan, Margaret Laurence, Sheila Watson, Stephen Leacock—are in the tributaries rather than the mainstream. And what is more, they are in the tributaries of American literature, not Canadian. Which does not mean, of course, that the work of these authors has any less literary merit. Indeed, in terms of universality of theme and appeal it could mean, and in some cases has meant, the very opposite. The mainstream is a matter of sphere of consciousness, not artistic skill, although sometimes the latter can be conditioned by the former.

With each passing year, more and more English-speaking writers are being drawn into the Canadian mainstream. Hugh Hood, in his sketches, stories and novels, is an obvious example, as are James Bacque and Ellis Portal mentioned earlier in this essay. Less obvious, perhaps, but nevertheless writing from a sphere of consciousness which includes all of Canada and in addition draws a great deal of outside experience into the distillation process of that sphere, are Dave Godfrey and Leonard Cohen.

So far as French-Canadian writers are concerned, until recently the great majority have been caught up in the various Québec tributaries of Canadian literature. In other words, they have been regional in spirit as well as setting. Lately, however, a number of authors—Jacques Renaud, André Major, Roch Carrier for example—have embraced spheres of consciousness which, like those of many of their anglophone colleagues, are more or less extensions of spheres already defined in the United States. But these writers and others such as Gérard Bessette, Réjean Ducharme, Aquin, Jasmin and Godbout, by virtue of a broadening awareness which includes English Canada to varying degrees, are moving definitely toward the Canadian mainstream. As their awareness shifts from the general implications of English-speaking America to the particular implications of English-speaking Canada, they will enter the mainstream more and more.

Hugh MacLennan, on the other hand, is already there. Provided that Canada continues to exist as a single nation, he may well be creating for himself a special status. I suspect that the day will come when Hugh MacLennan is considered to occupy a position much like that of Mark Twain in the United States, as the prime mover in the emergence of a distinctive Canadian literature.

Return of the Sphinx provides a panoramic view of the different kinds of Separatism. Daniel Ainslie, son of the protagonist, becomes a would-be terrorist. Like the heroes of Aquin and Jasmin, he is a failure, and for the same reasons. He cannot make a positive identification of the enemy, his problem being especially complex in view of mixed ancestry and a father who is Minister of Cultural Affairs in the federal government. A weakness in *Return of the Sphinx* is that MacLennan's characterization of Daniel is incomplete. The young man is believable enough, particularly after one has examined the supporting evidence in *Prochain épisode* and *Ethel et le terroriste*. But the characterization of Daniel lacks the psychological penetration and necessary intricacy of the portraits of terrorists by Aquin and Jasmin. Comparatively speaking, Daniel is a skeleton. The trouble, it would appear, is that Hugh MacLennan, despite considerable power of empathy, cannot sufficiently withdraw from the regions of sweetness and light. With regard to Daniel, the author is at his most effective in the scene where Marielle, a mature, passionate and attractive emigrée from Algeria, introduces the young man to the delights of physical love, while at the same time from her own experiences making him painfully aware of the bitter harvests of hatred.

Aimé Latendresse in *Return of the Sphinx* is an example of the second variety of Separatism, and he is presented quite sympathetically and convincingly. Like René Lévesque, he makes a lot of sense when he speaks of the disadvantages and humiliations long endured by French Canadians and the absolute need for new confidence and self-respect, for simple dignity. But in all fairness it must be said that MacLennan gives Latendresse an attitude much more sinister than any ever indicated by René Lévesque himself, although it is identical to that of certain other independentists. Latendresse, as might be expected, is a *prêtre manqué.* At another time, in another age, his energies and intellect would have been quietly expended within the greystone walls of a *collège classique* nestled at the outskirts of a small town. But now, like many of his counterparts in real life, he is at large, a man with an undeniable sense of mission coupled to a knowledge of history and great cunning. Here is no mongoloid misfit about to place a bomb in a mail box. Yet because of the sincerity and determination arising from his sense of mission, Latendresse is not above manipulating others to do what he might not do himself. If the means serves the end, he will not question it too deeply. "I sincerely hope so," he replies, when asked if independence can be achieved without bloodshed. But then he adds, "In the entire history of the human race, has that ever happened?" (p. 131) Marielle tells Daniel that Latendresse is an evil man. But that is because she—and one suspects that Hugh MacLennan feels the same

128

way—is convinced that anyone who would endorse a cause which is likely to lead to hatred, bloodshed and misery has got to be evil. Latendresse, however, is only evil inasmuch as the great majority of the world's leaders, revered and unrevered, have been evil; that is to say, having dedicated himself to an end, he is willing to grant that a certain number of individuals must be sacrificed to achieve that end.

Daniel's Uncle Ephrem provides an example of our third kind of Separatism. Chantal tells Gabriel of his views: " 'This is a good thing, this movement. It's the first thing that's ever made *les Anglais* squirm.' But I tell you Gabriel, that if the Queen visited Québec tomorrow Uncle Ephrem would probably be in command of the guard of honour, and if he wasn't he'd be furiously angry." (p. 46)

It is Joe Lacombe, however, the R.C.M.P. officer and former Air Force buddy of Alan Ainslie, who expresses the fourth brand of Separatism, and he does so in a way quite similar to that of the heroes in the French-Canadian novels we have discussed. Contradicting the ancient Québec dictum dramatized in *Maria Chapdelaine* — "Rien ne changera" — Lacombe says:

Ca change! Ca change! And the feeling's wonderful. Tabernacle, haven't we suffered enough? Supported enough for more than two hundred years? Prayed enough? Gone to mass often enough? Given the Church enough? Taken the lousiest jobs and eaten pea soup long enough because there were too many mouths to feed on much else except once a week and sometimes not even that often? Why should it always be us to carry the load for everyone? Be tired all the time like *sa mère*, smile like *sa mère* because there wasn't anything else she could afford to do? Work for the English boss all the time like P'pa, speaking English always to him in our own home? Or suppose we want to work in our own *milieu*—what then? In some dirty way with our own dirtiest politicians because they were the ones the English always liked because if they took money they knew they had them, took money under the counter and then did the opposite to what they promised the people who voted for them? Why can't we be free and clean and proud of ourselves? Why can't we succeed as French Canadians and not as imitations of the English and Americans? Why should they be the ones to judge whether we're any good or not? Why can't we judge that ourselves? (p. 104)

Return of the Sphinx thus echoes the message of *Prochain épisode* and *Ethel et le terroriste*. What is more important, however, is the novel's additional dimension, the observations MacLennan makes on English-Canadian attitudes. At the beginning of *Return of the Sphinx*, we are introduced to Herbert Tarnley, the prototype of the Anglo-Canadian businessman. Tarnley, of course, is concerned about only one thing—the security of his investments. MacLennan shows him with a curious, yet typical duality: through various informants he has a good idea of what is happening in French Canada and he is obviously worried; at the same time he can state categorically that if an independent Québec were to try to nationalize industry, she "would find herself an appendage on the Latin American desk of the State Department [Washington]." (p. 23) Tarnley, like so many of his counterparts in real life, is clearly a dynamic, capable man, the sort of person one would want to organize a blood drive or charity campaign. He believes in solutions, and his solution for the unrest in Québec is that the authorities should be firm and show no weakness. Clearly everyone benefits from a stable society; therefore Québec should be maintained as such. Tarnley's great deficiency is that he cannot understand spiritual and psychological aspirations. He is incapable of communicating with his son, but he does him the precious service of having his paintings evaluated by experts to establish that the boy has no artistic talent. When Ainslie is more or less kicked out of the government, Tarnley offers to endow a college and make him president. In other words, he knows what is good for everyone; and when Herbert Tarnley has control everyone is going to get what is good for him whether he likes it or not. Tarnley and Latendresse are thus brothers under the skin; and if Latendresse is an evil man, then in the end Tarnley is equally evil. Neither of these men will solve the problems of Québec or Canada.

Nor will the mighty politician, Moses Bulstrode. Fearless, absolutely honest, competent, built like a bear and Bible-bred, Bulstrode is the epitome of all the old warrior values. He takes no nonsense from anyone— members of the opposition, shrewd businessmen like Tarnley, editors or college professors. His attitude to Québec is neatly summed up in a remark he makes to Ainslie: "What gives the French Canadians this idea they've had it so tough? . . . It was twenty times tougher in the Yukon than it ever was in Quebec." (p. 68) And looking at the situation in Bulstrode's terms, undoubtedly it was.

MacLennan makes clear that Bulstrode is far from being anti-French Canadian. Indeed, Moses Bulstrode sympathizes with the people of Québec who have suffered from the exploitation of Westmount financiers, whom he regards as ruthless and corrupt. But as a strict matter of principle Bulstrode refuses to believe that French Canada should be accorded any special consideration. And it is here that Hugh MacLennan puts his finger on the crux of the Canadian riddle. If Bulstrode were a political operator or opportunist, if he were pro-English or anti-French, if he were simply ignorant, then he would not constitute much of a threat. But he is none of these things, and I believe that he represents a dominant body of opinion in English Canada today. Sincere and dedicated to the admirable principle of equal treatment for all, Bulstrode will never accept or comprehend the subtle distinctions which put French Canadians in a special category. To his mind, the poor in Toronto slums or Newfoundland fishing villages are just as deserving of attention as the residents of St. Henri, and who can argue the point?

Return of the Sphinx as the title intimates, does not solve the Canadian riddle. Ainslie, who has struggled to create an *entente* between the English and French of Canada, ends up effectively excommunicated by both groups. In this novel MacLennan reverses the Odyssey pattern of his previous books—the hero returns to a house in disorder, but his wise Penelope, in this case Constance, dies when he needs her most, and his son is bent upon stirring up more disorder.

And we, gentle readers, are left with the question—will it really endure? Or from another viewpoint—should it endure? Or to become completely involved in the puzzle—how will Canada endure?

I am not a prophet, but I remain convinced that one can learn more about people and society from creative literature than from scientific reports. In MacLennan's story, Herbert Tarnley and Moses Bulstrode are obviously of the type of person who would never waste time reading fiction. Consequently, they get to know the facts, but they are unlikely to be attuned to the underlying fears, hopes and frustrations. And the one point which surfaces from the troubled waters of the novels of Aquin, Godbout, Gravel, Bacque, Jasmin and MacLennan is that the significant brand of Québec Separatism is precisely a matter of fears, hopes and frustrations. All six writers advance the thesis that Québec is psychologically sick. Bilingual civil servants and bilingual districts may salve a few of the superficial irritations, the skin diseases, but they will not cure the disturbed psyche.

Is there anything which can effect such a cure? Is there any way to instil self-confidence, a sense of cultural security and a feeling of dignity in the masses of French Canadians who have not actually committed themselves to the Separatist Movement? I think that there are certain moves which would have a definite remedial effect. For one thing, the egalitarian attitude represented by Bulstrode in *Return of the Sphinx* and apparently an entrenched principle of English-Canadian thinking must be modified. French Canadians, as the novels we have examined clearly illustrate, think of themselves first as a group or nation rather than as individuals. Thus the idea of equality does not have the same bearing in French Canada as in English Canada. In Québec, it signifies equal treatment for the French-Canadian nation—on a group basis rather than on an individual basis. What matters is how the French-Canadian collectivity is treated. In other words, French Canada as a whole must have a special status. And in the light of the psychological problems discussed in all the novels, such a special status, including the greatest degree of autonomy possible within a confederate system, makes sense.

But if a genuine feeling of cultural security is to be created once and for all in Québec, a cultural security which will make the novels we have examined historical documents instead of reflections of actuality, there is one vital step which must be taken—Québec must become an officially unilingual, French-language province. I can see no other way to create a sense of cultural security and to make French Canadians as a group equal to English Canadians. After all, the other nine provinces are essentially unilingual. Whatever the glories of bilingualism, so long as it smacks of necessary accommodation it will be regarded in Québec as a threat to the French language and to French-Canadian culture, as a step away from cultural security. To the average English Canadian, bilingualism means acquiring a second language; at the moment, to many French Canadians it means the likelihood of losing a first one. Yet, if through official unilingualism a sense of cultural security were to develop in French Canada, then the current linguistic tensions would undoubtedly diminish, and the result would be more genuine bilingualism than ever before. Right now, to French-speaking Quebeckers cultural security means more than ever the tourist dollar. Settle the problem of security, and the tourist dollar will take care of the rest. In short, ironic as it may seem, an officially unilingual Québec would be the greatest possible boost for Canadian bilingualism.

I might add that a unilingual Québec, legally instituted rather than forcefully imposed, need not present any danger or special inconvenience to English-speaking Quebeckers. According to the 1961 Census, nearly thirty per cent of them already speak French, compared with less than twenty-five per cent of French Canadians who speak English. Where English-Canadians are in sufficient numbers they should be permitted to maintain schools and other institutions, but with adequate and efficient teaching of French as a condition. And with more than half of the television channels seen in Québec already coming from over the American border, English-speaking Quebeckers are not going to develop a complex about the imminent disappearance of their mother tongue.

Now if Québec is to have special status amounting to virtual autonomy and if she is to become officially unilingual, why not go all the way and declare an independent nation? Do not these concessions amount to independence? In effect they do. But as agreed-upon concessions, they could be a means to avoid the hatred, violence and bloodshed which are described or suggested in each of the novels we have considered. They could be a means to avoid outright separation and the dangers of economic chaos, political anarchy and possible American intervention, against which even René Lévesque can offer no guarantees. In a conversation with his son, MacLennan's protagonist Alan Ainslie says: "Well, perhaps Quebec *will* separate. But if she does, let it be done decently. Let it be done without hatred and murder and all this paranoia of you and your friends." (p. 257) Special status and official unilingualism do not mean separation, but they are important steps Canada can take to relieve the malaise so vividly portrayed in the novels we have discussed. They are a means to foster the cultural and spiritual independence Québec clearly must have, an independence which French Canadians would thus be able to achieve decently.

Cornerstone for a New Morality

The Canadian novel has come a long way since William Kirby's golden dog and Gérin-Lajoie's perfect Christian farmer Jean Rivard. In both English and French the novel has moved from early historical romances and moral parables to stark realism and symbolic phantasy tinged with black humour. And in the course of this evolution it has reflected, whether directly or indirectly, the changing attitudes of Canadian society. Our best writers, like the best writers in any country, have had their finger on the collective pulse. For those who have eyes to see, they are the diagnosticians, the psycho-analysts and the prophets of the nation. And at a time like the present, when the nation is parading the symptoms of a grave sickness, we may do well to pay attention to what they have to say.

Since the end of the Second World War, significant Canadian novelists have been predominantly concerned with the disappearance of traditional values. Novelists everywhere, of course, have had the same concern, but it seems likely that in Canada, where the two major ethnic groups tried so long to outdo each other in conservatism, where the old values were so strongly entrenched and where literature was for a long time essentially a celebration of these values, the concern has been and continues to be greater and more agonizing than in most other countries. In recent years there has been a drastic shift in attitudes, a movement from one extreme to the other extreme. Québec, where once the hope for survival rested upon the twin principles of stubborn opposition to any change whatsoever and "la revanche du berceau"—the revenge of the cradle— Québec has turned to total obliteration of the old ways, to birth control and abortion, and for a few on the outer fringe the bombs and guns of the F.L.Q. "Où sont les neiges d'antan" and the Maria Chapdelaines who dutifully trudged through them? Maria—no bleeding heart she—knew exactly what she had to do. Except for a few moments of uncertainty, her decision as to what way of life to follow was never in doubt. Had she really opted to break with tradition, she would have been condemned by the society in which she lived and tormented by feelings of guilt. But there are no Maria Chapdelaines in the important novels of the post-war period. Even Florentine Lacasse, in Roy's *Bonheur d'occasion*, does not hesitate to use every means, including her body, to get what she wants. The one thing she is determined not to do is to follow in the footsteps of her mother. She, along with the protagonists of Hugh MacLennan, André Langevin, Marie-Claire Blais, Mordecai Richler or just about any contemporary novelist one might mention, desires to break with the past, to liberate herself as much as possible from the values of earlier generations.

In effect, the big difference between Canadian novels written before World War II and those which have appeared more recently is that in the latter the characters are not so much struggling against something external as they are struggling against themselves, and particularly against personal feelings of emptiness and indecision. The old moral standards which for centuries served as measuring sticks for the conduct of life, have all gone down the drain. Undoubtedly World War I, the great depression and various other events had something to do with the weakening of these traditional standards, but it was World War II which administered the *coup de grâce* demonstrating once and for all that codes of morality are superficial rather than fundamental. When the chips are down, they do not rate even lip service. Two novels which deal specifically with the war itself, Jean Vaillancourt's *Les Canadiens errants* and Colin McDougall's *Execution* provide a penetrating analysis of this phenomenon.

Both novels describe the reaction of Canadian soldiers to the brutality and horrors of military operations. The initial phase of this reaction is a blunting of the sensitivity—a person who remains normally sensitive to violence and killing will not be able to last long in a war. It is necessary to build a shell around oneself. Unfortunately, however, this shell is never perfect. In *Execution* there is an episode when the Canadian soldiers are in a barnyard with an old Italian farmer and his son. Suddenly a shell explodes, killing one of the soldiers and the farmer's son. The Canadians have already conditioned themselves to such happenings. The dead soldier's best friend is quietly ordered to collect his gun and personal effects. But then after a few moments of stunned silence, the old farmer begins to scream hysterically. "Mio bambino!" he cries to the heavens, "Morte! Morte!" And because the protective shell of the soldiers is not perfect, they cannot endure this demonstration of natural human despair. Finally, the farmer is silenced by a hard slap in the face. (p. 55 ff.) In *Les*

140

Canadiens errants, Vaillancourt depicts the reaction of a hardened veteran in this way: "Lanthier le contempla sans rien dire. Même les soldats les plus endurcis comme lui ne s'habituaient jamais tout à fait à la mort. Le capitaine Beauvais était le premier mort de la journée." (p. 102)

Neither McDougall nor Vaillancourt is interested in singing the heroics of war. There are no thin red lines or charges of the light brigade in these novels. In fact, the two books clearly illustrate that men confronted with brutality are invariably reduced to perpetrating the same kind of brutality. In other words, war can force a man to discover the bestiality within himself, which might well have remained hidden all his life under the normal conditions of a reasonably tranquil and conventional society. In a war, everyman can become a Kurtz. When for example, a German prisoner spits in the face of Lanthier, one of Vaillancourt's characters, he can no longer control himself:

"Ah, mon enfant-de-chienne!" he hissed. He had grabbed his Sten by the strap, breaking a branch off a tree as he swung it through the air. He smashed it into the face of his insulter, knocking him to the ground. Lanthier pointed the barrel at the man's chest and pressed the trigger until the clip was empty. The German's body quivered, then for a few moments went through a hideous convulsion, twisting like a worm. Finally it lay still.[23]

In McDougall's *Execution* there are a number of similar incidents. In short, for a man to be a competent soldier in battle he must also be an efficient killer. And this bitter realization sooner or later leads the more philosophical natures to a redefinition of traditional values, of the hallowed notions of courage, goodness, justice, decency and mercy. The soldiers in both

Execution and *Les Canadiens errants* begin to question the principles of the Christian religion they had been taught to accept as children. Richard Lanoue, in Vaillancourt's book, is a skilled and capable fighting man who hangs on to his beliefs for a period of time. But finally his faith is shaken. "Que pensait Dieu," he speculates, "si Dieu voyait les malheureuses créatures qu'il soumettait à cette épreuve inhumaine? Dieu s'était moqué cruellement du courage des hommes qui était la meilleure chose en eux. Leur dignité unique. Il l'avait ironiquement écrasé sous une montagne pour le détruire. Maintenant, Richard était brisé, sa vie n'avait plus de sens." (p. 139)

Colin McDougall provides a dramatic illustration of how the most solid kind of Christian faith can be destroyed with his character Philip Doorn, a military chaplain. When Doorn disembarks with the army in Sicily, he sincerely believes that he is God's agent accompanying a band of crusaders. He is filled with enthusiasm and exultation. He is the Church Militant. But then he witnesses the realities of war. And the biggest shock for Padre Doorn is that he begins to apprehend that his Canadian crusaders are just as capable of cruelty and butchery as are the "pagan Huns." Padre Doorn finally comes to the conclusion that God somehow must be unaware of what is going on. Surely a just God, the God of his childhood and seminary days, would never permit such depraved activities and insane annihilation to take place. Deciding to bring the matter to God's attention, he steals a piece of wood said to be part of the true cross and carries it with him onto a battlefield. While the shells are bursting around him, he holds the precious relic in the air. But nothing happens. The battle continues. And the piece of the true cross is ground into dust along with the rest of the debris. (p. 12)

For many participants, then, the war creates an

existential vacuum—a frame of mind in which all values
have lost their validity. The vacuum can be temporarily
counteracted by unthinking, total concentration on a
function, which is the course initially followed by John
Adam, Richard Lanoue and several others in the two
war novels. Eventually, however, the existential vacuum
exhibits itself in extreme cynicism and the attitude that
the world is entirely devoid of meaning and purpose,
offering only momentary periods of peace through
oblivion. Vaillancourt's *Les Canadiens errants* closes
with an effective dramatization of this attitude:

> At one o'clock, Richard gave la Minoune another
> five-dollar bill. He had forgotten the war.
>
> At two o'clock, he gave her another bill. He had
> forgotten the war and after the war.
>
> At three o'clock, he gave her the last bill in his wallet.
> He had forgotten the war, after the war, life, and
> himself. As for la Minoune, she seemed to have
> forgotten the St. George Café.[24]

It is notable that Vaillancourt's novel ends with the
implication that "la Minoune," who has not been in the
war, is living in more or less the same existential vacuum
as the veteran Lanoue. In other words, the dissolution
of the old system of values was accentuated by the war,
and as we have seen, the process of dissolution can
perhaps be most clearly discerned in certain war novels,
but the phenomenon is by no means limited to the
military. Once the existential vacuum has been noted
and defined, an examination of other Canadian novels
written during the post-war period reveals that in
various disguises it is in fact widespread.

In the most recent fiction—books which have
appeared since about 1960—total absence of traditional
social and moral values is standard. In Bessette's *La*

Bagarre, Cohen's *Beautiful Losers*, Godbout's *Le Couteau sur la table*, Le Pan's *The Deserter*, Symons' *Place d'Armes*, Renaud's *Le Cassé*, Major's *Cabochon*, to mention a few examples, the characters begin at absolute zero, often looking for something, looking for anything which might bring meaning and a sense of direction to their lives, "waiting for Godot," as Beckett has put it. For example, Québec Separatism, drugs, thrill killings, rock festivals, nudism, pornography, even the F.L.Q.—all these things can provide for certain people a kind of direction or a kind of oblivion, with varying results. In the latest fiction, as in the lives of the youth of today, more often than not the oblivion principle is dominant. Richard Lanoue finds himself a somewhat basic and simple instrument of oblivion—a whore from the St. George Café. In recent fiction, however, the effect is accomplished by all manner of elaborate means to heighten sensual experience to the point where the mind is blotted out, transcended. In a way it is Transcendentalism all over again, but without the philosophical hangover and with amplifiers to magnify the vibrations. And there is no question of tuning in to the Over-Soul—one tunes in to oneself and hears the heartbeat of the tribe. Which, come to think about it, is probably what Emerson, Wordsworth, Thoreau and the others were driving at anyway. They confused the issues by trying too hard to accommodate the highlights of three thousand previous years of philosophical and theological musings.

The contemporary fad of the discotheque provides an intriguing illustration of the oblivion principle. Music is played at a volume which precludes conversation or even thought, space is limited, confining rather than expanding the senses, lighting is minimal and constantly changing, no handsome couple with fancy footwork discourages anyone from feeling part of the action, the dancing itself consists of movements suggestive of copulation, but without the complications, challenges and private, group-excluding emotions of actual body contact. Total, mind-smothering group involvement. And novels such as Leonard Cohen's *Beautiful Losers*, whether we like what it is saying or not, faithfully capture the spirit of the age, complete with existential vacuum and oblivion release. When there is any attempt at all to evaluate the experience of living, the old distinction between moral and immoral is abandoned in favour of an attempt to distinguish between the authentic and the false. But the attempt invariably fails from the lack of an objective standard. The individual depends completely on himself; thus anything can happen, and all kinds of bizarre events are described in the novels of the 1960s. If we go back to the post-war period before 1960, on the other hand, the majority of novels are concerned with a confrontation between the traditional values and the new absence of values. And it seems to me that an important key to the understanding of more recent works can be found in an examination of this confrontation.

The confrontation can be seen in the works of Roger Lemelin, Yves Thériault, André Langevin, Robert Elie, and especially, so far as the French-Canadian novel is concerned, in Gabrielle Roy's *Bonheur d'occasion* and Jean Simard's *Mon Fils pourtant heureux*. Hugh MacLennan, Adele Wiseman, Mordecai Richler, John Marlyn and W. O. Mitchell are among those English-speaking writers who treat the same theme. In *Bonheur d'occasion* and in Wiseman's *The Sacrifice*, the tragic results of adherence to an obsolete system of values are illustrated with particular poignancy. Roy's Rose-Anna Lacasse finds herself in the Montreal slum of St. Henri with a big family and an unemployed husband. Yet she continues to live according to the old rural practices. Believing that it would be sinful to use contraception, she produces a child every spring regularly; and regularly every spring, because the rent cannot be paid, along with thousands of other slum dwellers she must find another flat. But Rose-Anna does not rebel or complain. If her life is hard, she knows exactly why: she is enduring her *purgatoire sur terre*. It is understood that her reward will come in the hereafter. She has a few moments of doubt as to the extent of God's interest in her affairs—"la seule fêlure dans sa foi venait de cette candide supposition que Dieu, distrait, fatigué, harassé comme elle, en arrivait à ne plus accorder qu'une attention éparse aux besoins humains." (p. 89) But she remains convinced of the necessity for *la résignation chrétienne* even when her baby son dies and her family is disintegrating before her eyes.

Wiseman's *The Sacrifice* is one of the rare Canadian novels in English as effective and powerful as *Bonheur d'occasion*. The protagonist, an immigrant butcher from the Ukraine called Abraham, is an even more tragic figure than Rose-Anna Lacasse. Before his arrival in the Canadian West, he had witnessed the brutal murder of his two sons, Moses and Jacob, during a pogrom. Abraham is an orthodox Jew, and like Rose-Anna he is ready to endure all tribulations rather than modify his attitude toward the role of man on the earth. Consequently, his remaining son Isaac, like the Lacasse children, adopts a philosophy of life which is quite different from that of his parents. He wishes to adapt to the realities around him. A conflict arises, for instance, when Isaac and his wife Ruth want their baby to be born in a hospital, and Abraham, because such an act would be a break with tradition, is dead set against the idea. The old man, of course, had concentrated all his hopes and dreams in Isaac, his only surviving son; thus the latter is the subject of greater expectations than he might otherwise have been. But this only complicates the situation and creates greater tension between father and son when Isaac refuses to conform to the beliefs

and ideals of his father. Nevertheless, Abraham adores
Isaac, and Isaac has much respect and affection for
Abraham. When the family synagogue catches fire,
Isaac rushes into the building and saves the holy Torah,
despite a heart ailment. But the tremendous strain takes
its toll, and after a few months of illness he dies.
Abraham, who has also lost his wife shortly before, is a
broken man. He still has his daughter-in-law Ruth and his
grandson Moses, but Ruth is even less inclined than Isaac
to accept the pattern of life dictated by Abraham, and
inevitable disputes occur over the education of the child.

It is during this period of despair that Abraham's
employer asks him to deliver a package of meat to
Laiah, a lady of easy virtue who has always had an eye
for the still-robust butcher. When she was a young girl in
Europe, Laiah had been raped by a bearded Russian
landlord, and Abraham's maturity and full beard pro-
voke perverse sexual desire in her. On several occasions
she has already tried to attract his attention, offering
him cakes and cups of tea whenever he came to deliver
meat, but always without reaction. She makes the
mistake, however, of mounting the big play at a time
when Abraham, after a violent quarrel with his
daughter-in-law, is in a state of absolute depression and
confusion. At that moment in the eyes of Laiah,
Abraham is a desirable male, a male who seems at last to
be responding to her charms; in the eyes of Abraham
the woman becomes the very incarnation of evil and sin
in the world.

She, a depraved Jezebel, barren, lascivious, the
veritable antithesis of all he holds to be sacred, is alive,
while his three sons, his wife, his hopes and his dreams,
all that he has expended his life and his energies for, are
dead. What provokes Abraham is not sexual desire, but
the wrath of an upright man, a mighty wrath which
total frustration has pushed to the point of temporary
madness. And unfortunately for Laiah, a freshly honed

carving knife is on the table nearby. Repeating to himself the word "Life," Abraham, butcher by trade, cuts the woman's throat with professional expertise. (p. 293 ff.)

The court decides that Abraham is insane, and he is sent to an asylum. Several years later when Moses is visiting his grandfather, he discovers that the old man's attitudes have changed. He is no longer convinced that he is in a position to make moral judgements or that he has a hot line to God and the unique truth. But the change has come too late.

What Rose-Anna and Abraham (before the final change) have in common, of course, is the conviction that their beliefs are the exclusive will of God. And each has the courage of this conviction. The problem described in both novels is that alterations in the conditions of life require corresponding alterations in the conduct and attitudes of people. Rose-Anna and Abraham, incapable of making the necessary adjustments, become tragic figures, alienated not only from contemporary society but also from their immediate families. They themselves do not experience the existential vacuum, but their lives exemplify the futility of hanging onto values no longer adapted to the realities of life. Awareness of this futility causes those less perversely dedicated than Rose-Anna and Abraham to abandon the old values, and as the traditional codes tumble, the existential vacuum establishes itself. The children of the two families react to the tragic lives of their parents in much the same way as the soldiers in *Execution* and *Les Canadiens errants* react to the war.

This reaction, naturally, does not mean that they will find happiness. It is probable that those who adhered strictly to the Old Order, whether Jewish, Christian or other, were happier. They knew what they had to do and what they had to avoid, and they acted accordingly. They knew how to resign themselves to life.

This very resignation, however, is undoubtedly one of the important reasons why in a world which has witnessed such a phenomenal increase in material goods over the last century, there has been so little social progress. Understandably enough, the well-off and established people have had no difficulty resigning themselves to being well-off and established. They can be counted upon to support the establishment and to resist change. But the poor have become poorer, and the helpless have become even more helpless, or at least more conscious of their helplessness. The Rose-Annas and Abrahams, no matter how much we may admire their tenacity and integrity, have been too willing to accept their "purgatories on earth." In fact, they expected nothing better. And since they did not demand a share of the benefits of the world's material progress, naturally they did not receive any. They were the domestic animals of the affluent society. And just as a curious combination of temperance fanatics and mobsters brought about Prohibition in the U.S.A., these people have combined with the well-off and established to impede necessary social change. But contemporary society, where the Rose-Annas and Abrahams are an ever-decreasing minority, a society unrestrained by Christian, Jewish or any other kind of resignation, is now presenting its list of demands, and with increasingly violent determination. The relatively placid days of the Old Order are gone forever. And there are some who are not satisfied only to rock the boat—they would like to sink it.

The traditional system of values of the western world, however, did something more than simply condition people to accept their lot. It furnished individuals with a convenient *raison d'être*, a pattern supposedly divine into which one could fit. And if the new generation is seeking to increase its portion of the good things of the world, it is also seeking, whether consciously or not,

something to replace the old *raison d'être*. This vital
quest, in fact, traverses the barriers between the haves
and the have-nots, between the drop-outs and the
stay-ins, and between cultures, languages and religions.
In Jean Simard's *Mon Fils pourtant heureux* and Hugh
MacLennan's *The Watch That Ends the Night*, it is
effectively dramatized.

Mon Fils pourtant heureux is an iconoclastic novel.
The opening line—"Je me nomme Fabrice Navarin"—
recalls the beginning of another, much more famous
iconoclastic novel, *Moby Dick*. Simard tells the story of
a man brought up in a conventional, middle-class
Québec family. As a child Fabrice acquires the values of
his ethnic group in the same manner as do the majority
of children. He learns how to pray: "Il m'arrivait même,
certains matins, de prier avec abandon, la ferveur
confuse d'un enfant trop seul qui trouve soudain à Qui
parler, bousculant les oraisons, sollicitant pêle-mêle les
faveurs du ciel et les bienfaits terrestres; une bicyclette
et le salut éternel" (p. 13)—a bicycle and eternal
salvation! Like Holden Caulfield in Salinger's *Catcher in
the Rye* and many other young characters in contemporary fiction, Simard's protagonist insists on
questioning everything and on rejecting what he finds
false or artificial. He examines the ideas of his mother,
his father, his grandmother, and subjects his own mind
to severe self-analysis. In the process, one after another
the values fall.

Fabrice is particularly bitter about the French-
Canadian system of education, which, to his mind,
aimed at conserving the *status quo* by stifling
independent thought and the desire for any kind of
change. Speaking of the classical colleges for boys, now
almost a thing of the past although certain aspects linger
on to this day, he states: "L'enfant sortait de là avec la
certitude d'être habité par des passions immondes,
menacé de mort prochaine et destiné à un jugement

impitoyable—à moins, bien entendu, qu'il ne devienne
l'émule des saints personnages inhumés sous la chapelle,
et proposés à son imitation." (p. 108) Simard, of course,
knew what he was talking about, and numerous other
authors have provided supporting evidence for this
adverse view. It is no wonder, then, that the Old Order
in Québec has split at the seams so quickly; nor is it
surprising that the "quiet revolution" has become so
noisy at times.

The tone of Simard's book strongly suggests that not
only the educational system, but the whole of French-
Canadian society was organized in such a way as to
militate against any possibility of social progress. He
speaks of "la graine janséniste" and shows how the
notion is sown that one is supposed to suffer on earth.
"De quels tristes mariages," he asks, "entre puritains et
jansénistes cette fausse austérité n'est-elle pas née, qui
pervertit chez nous tant de rapports humains, toutes nos
joies?" (p. 58)

But Fabrice's awareness of the weaknesses in his
society does not supply him with a remedy. Like
Abraham in *The Sacrifice*, he becomes a solitary man
alienated from his own people, except that after having
tossed out all the conventional values, he has no
convictions left to fall back on. Toward the end of the
novel he has reached the point where life appears to be
completely senseless, the point reached by Richard
Lanoue in *Les Canadiens errants*.

At that time, however, Fabrice chances to meet
Albert, an employee of the small Paris hotel where he is
staying. At first, he cannot understand this new
acquaintance. Fabrice has had a relatively comfortable
existence and many opportunities; yet he is bitter about
life, demoralized, contemplating suicide. Albert, on the
other hand, has suffered every imaginable knock—after
having worked his way out of the slums he had lost
everything in the war and had been thrown into a

concentration camp. Yet Albert has a contagious good humour, a *joie de vivre*. He is confident and happy to be alive, willing to make the best of what each day offers.

Because of the influence of Albert's sunny nature and spontaneous sympathy Fabrice finally regains his will to live, after everything else, including a long confession with a clergyman friend, has failed. In effect, Albert teaches him two things: the first is that injustice and misery will always exist in the world; it is foolish to imagine that man's inhumanity to man is going to stop or even become significantly less. But the fact that one must accept its imperfections does not justify the rejection of life itself. To avoid the problem by the explanation that misery is one's *purgatoire sur terre* amounts to rejection, perhaps the most sinister kind of rejection. One can accept the imperfections of life on earth without at the same time resolving that one should not struggle for improvement, without concluding that there is no possibility or necessity for conditions to be better. Albert, by a simple act of sympathy for another human being, improves his own life and that of the other man. The second principle which Fabrice discovers, then, is that one must retain the capacity to love, to have sympathy for others. Thus it is possible to abandon the whole superstructure of traditional morality, but in accepting the often crude reality, in accepting life just as it is while at the same time retaining the capacity to love, one can create a new and effective *raison d'être*: "Le secret, c'est qu'il n'y a pas de secret! Albert est heureux parce qu'il vit, voilà tout: il est en vie, il est dans la vie . . . . La vie est difficile, souvent, terrifiante, parfois intenable. Mais elle est bonne." (p. 227)

MacLennan's *The Watch that Ends the Night* comes to exactly the same conclusion as *Mon Fils pourtant heureux*. The book's protagonist, George Stewart, is conditioned as a child by an authoritarian aunt quite similar to the grandmother of Fabrice Navarin. George meets his future wife, Catherine, while he is still a boy, but the girl is suffering from a heart ailment, and his aunt warns him not to become involved. Catherine has already been told by doctors that she cannot expect to have a normal life, and that certainly she will never be able to risk having a baby. But the girl is stubborn and defiant. Generously endowed with beauty and talent, she is determined to live her life to the fullest degree possible. On one occasion, for instance, she attempts to make George a gift of her naked young body; ironically, her attempt at seduction fails, not because of a lack of desire and affection on George's part but because his affection is so strong that he cannot take the risk of putting the girl's health in danger. Catherine then decides to go her own way, and eventually she meets the dynamic, idealistic doctor Jerome Martel. Jerome does not hesitate to take the risk George had declined, and since his personality permits him to inspire confidence in Catherine, her baby is delivered without great strain. The two marry and remain reasonably happy until Jerome decides to go to Spain to serve the socialist cause.

In *The Watch that Ends the Night* MacLennan describes how for many people the ideals of socialism provided a temporary substitute for the disappearing Old Order. Jerome, as we have noted, is an idealist. He is presumably convinced that the world can be changed, and that a new and equitable distribution of materials and benefits can be effected if only the capitalist system, together with Fascism, can be destroyed. George, on the other hand, is a confused individual and essentially uncommitted. He has not been able to embrace any cause with enthusiasm; as a result he has become increasingly demoralized as life to him appears to become more and more absurd. He has, however, kept his capacity to love, and this is precisely the force that sustains him. When Jerome has disappeared and is officially declared dead, Catherine finally accepts George as her husband. By that time she is helpless, but George, despite the fact that he knows she still loves Jerome, takes it upon himself to care for her and her daughter Sally.

Never having imagined that the world could become a utopia, George can survive when the dreams evaporate and he is left on his own resources, for these resources include a willingness to accept life as it is and a capacity to love. Thus when Jerome miraculously reappears, George can endure the experience of witnessing how his wife has never stopped loving the husband who had abandoned her. For George, as for Fabrice, it is more important to love than to be loved. And the act of emotional involvement allows both these men to avoid the desperate cynicism, the existential vacuum of Richard Lanoue in *Les Canadiens errants*.

To return to the war novels for a moment, it is of interest here to note that McDougall strikes the same positive note as Simard and MacLennan. In this respect *Execution* contrasts sharply with *Les Canadiens errants*. McDougall's protagonist, John Adam, is able to escape the existential vacuum through a chance encounter with an Italian girl. The girl, like so many others at the time, has been forced into prostitution in order to keep her family from starving. But to maintain a modicum of self-respect and to avoid complete despair, she has developed a system of pretence. She makes believe that she is with a true lover rather than with any stranger who might have the necessary cash. Accordingly, she asks Adam to repeat the words *Io ti amo*—I love you—before taking her. For such a beautiful young thing at a cheap price, it seems little to ask; but Adam, in the depths of cynicism, is enraged by the request. Why should this girl be allowed to pretend that life is better than it is. Like Richard Lanoue's "La Minoune,"

154

the female body on the bed can provide him with a short period of oblivion—that is all he wants. Yet the obvious pain his blunt refusal has caused the girl is disturbing for him. After a few moments of hesitation he learns that despite the protective shell he had built around himself, he is still capable of compassion. He repeats the words *Io ti amo*, and in so doing he grasps the truth imparted to Fabrice by Albert. The girl's request, even though it is in the fragile framework of pretence, indicates that she has refused to be reduced to nothing and to abandon life as meaningless. From then on Adam develops a new attitude, the courage to face life and to become emotionally involved.[25] Later, when he is forced to take part in the execution of an innocent soldier, this attitude is reinforced, and he discovers a profound sympathy for his fellow human beings: "Each one of them, in his fashion, was a good man. The trouble was that they *were* men, and being such, they were caught up in the strangling nets which man's plight cast over them: they could not always act the way their goodness wanted them to." (p. 227) There is, however, in men and in life always the possibility of goodness.

Considering the whole range of significant Canadian novels since the 1940s, then, four distinct attitudes toward life can be discerned. The two extremes alluded to at the beginning of this essay are, of course, religious resignation and the existential vacuum. Between these extremes are found idealism—the belief that the faults of the world can be removed by some miraculous social change—and the final philosophy adopted by Fabrice, George and John Adam. This philosophy, unfettered by metaphysical overtones and sanctioned by man's real and basic need to survive rather than by a hypothetical divine fiat, might perhaps be labelled "realistic involvement." But whatever the label, it is simply the willingness to accept life as it is and to struggle for any possible improvement through sympathy and love for other human beings.

Now without doubt it is the existential vacuum which is currently haunting the forefront of literary consciousness, faithfully reflecting the situation in life itself. As I mentioned earlier, novels written since 1960 almost exclusively adopt a negative and pessimistic stance. In contrast to Fabrice, George and Adam, the heroes or anti-heroes of these novels do not finally succeed in finding a way to accept and integrate the world around them. For the most part they are presented as sensitive and honest, and they are quite legitimately repelled by the corruption, ruthlessness and hypocrisy they see in society. Moreover, they see correctly. The flaws are surely there. But beneath the surface irritations, when these characters are not being sidetracked by the oblivion principle, they are searching painfully for a vital truth, for a rationale which will somehow sprout a workable *raison d'être*.

What intrigues me about this whole business, however, is that quite possibly the vital truth has already been found. It seems to me that the older modern novelists—MacLennan, Simard and McDougall—have hit something so simple and fundamental that perhaps even they have not realized its full significance. Certainly the younger writers provide a more striking picture of the existential vacuum. But that is all they do. And the existential vacuum, after all, is just that—a state of nothingness. The mental state itself cannot long continue, and its aspects, moods and variations can be recorded for only so long. It would appear that there is no question of returning to the Old Order. That has gone the way of the horse and buggy. It is equally clear, however, that the frustration and emptiness which must perforce accompany the deterioration of long-established directive values in life, cannot long endure. Western society will have to rebuild a structure of social and moral values—a new morality—and the simple principle of "realistic involvement" outlined by Hugh MacLennan, Jean Simard and Colin McDougall may well be the cornerstone required.

Note on Translation and Comparative Studies in Canada

Comparative Canadian Literature as disciplined literary analysis is still in its infancy. But there have been isolated instances in the past of individuals attempting at least to create preliminary bridges between the literatures of Canada's two major ethnic groups. I have already observed the vital relationship of translation to comparative studies. Not long ago, in an article in *Meta*, the translator and critic Philip Stratford commented on the dearth of good translations of Canadian Literature. He went on to call for greatly increased activity in the field, describing it as "not a second-rate occupation," but " . . . exhilarating, fascinating and creative." Fortunately, there are a number of people who are now taking up Stratford's challenge. Encouragement of translation, however, is not a phenomenon of long standing in Canada.

Among the most impressive of pioneering translation efforts in this country is the French version of Rosanna

Eleanor Leprohon's period romance, *The Manor House of Villerai* (1859), which was produced by E. L. de Bellefeuille under the title *Le Manoir de Villerai* in 1861. Other serial novels written by Mrs. Leprohon (née Mullins), which are set in Québec and contain detailed descriptions of French-Canadian customs of the time, were translated into French by a J. Genaud. In 1864 appeared the first English version of the long, still fascinating novel called *Les anciens Canadiens*, written by Philippe-Joseph Aubert de Gaspé when he was 73 years old and, like François-Xavier Garneau, had been stung to the quick by Lord Durham's storied indictment of French Canadians as a people without a history or a literature. (Recalling the likewise stimulating effects of a British critic's remark about the non-existence of an American literature, one wonders what might have happened if some foreign observer had made insulting comments on English-Canadian writing.) *Canadians of Old* was the title of the 1864 translation of Aubert de Gaspé's book by Georgina M. Penée, and the same title was used by Charles G. D. Roberts when he brought out his version in 1890. Penée's work was later reprinted under the new title of *Seigneur d'Haberville* in 1905, and the Roberts translation as *Cameron of Lochiel* in 1927. Thus this one particular book has come to be known by four different names.

Other notable early translations are Pamphile Lemay's *Le Chien d'or* (1884) from William Kirby's *The Golden Dog*, and William McLennan's *Songs of Old Canada*, a collection of renditions of French-Canadian *chansons*, which appeared in 1886. At the turn of the century, the prominent Québec writer Louis-Honoré Fréchette, a man who himself needed no cultural bridge, brought out a French version of his own *Christmas in French Canada*, which so far as I can determine he had originally written in English and published in 1899 in Toronto. It is interesting to note, incidentally, that in a country with so many bilingual people, very few authors have ever attempted, as apparently did Fréchette, to write and publish in both languages. Two other exceptions to the rule are James MacPherson Le Moine, a Québec City lawyer whose works include *Les Pêcheries du Canada* (1863) and *Maple Leaves* (six volumes, 1863-1906), a series of short sketches on local history and legend, and the more celebrated Marius Barbeau, who has produced numerous volumes on and of folklore, folksongs and legends. The material in Barbeau's *Folksongs of Old Quebec* (1935), nevertheless, was translated by Regina Lenore Schoolman, and his recent volume *Jongleur Songs of Old Quebec* (1962) has translations by Harold Boulton and Ernest MacMillan.

To return to the pioneers, almost as if to make up for the paucity of translations in Canada and outdoing even the treatment of Aubert de Gaspé's *Les anciens Canadiens*, two separate English versions of Louis Hémon's *Maria Chapdelaine* appeared at the same time in 1921. Andrew MacPhail did one, but the rendition which has rightfully endured is that of William Hume Blake. Actually, Blake did much more than this to improve inter-cultural understanding in Canada. His *Brown Waters and Other Sketches* (1915) and *In a Fishing Country* (1922) were written expressly to acquaint English-speaking people with Québec customs and attitudes. In addition, he translated Adjutor Rivard's *Chez Nous* under the title of *Chez Nous—Our Old Quebec Home* (1924).

A number of collections of poetry have presented French-speaking and English-speaking Canadian writers together. Bliss Carman and Lorne Pierce led the way with their anthology *Our Canadian Literature: Representative Verse, English and French*, first published in 1922 and enlarged in 1923. Selections of verse in French were included in *A Book of Canadian Prose and*

Verse (1923) edited by E. K. and Eleanor H. Broadus. Professor Watson Kirkconnell provided English translations for Séraphin Marion's anthology of French-Canadian poems entitled *Tradition du Québec/The Quebec Tradition*, which appeared in 1946. Twelve years later another parallel-text edition was published by G. R. Roy, *Twelve Modern French-Canadian Poets/ Douze poètes modernes du Canada français*. In the sixties, both French and English poets have been represented in A. J. M. Smith's *The Oxford Book of Canadian Verse*, Eli Mandel and Jean-Guy Pilon's *Poetry 62* and Jacques Godbout and John Robert Colombo's *Poesie/Poetry 64*. Louis Dudek provides translations of Québec poets in his *Poetry of Our Time*, as does John Glassco, who earlier rendered the *Journal of Saint-Denys Garneau* (1962), in his *The Poetry of French Canada in Translation* (1970). Selections from the works of individual authors have been translated into English by the team of Jean Beaupré and Gail Turnbull, by F. R. Scott and by P. E. Widdows, and in 1969 the quarterly *Ellipse*, with parallel-text presentations of both English-Canadian and French-Canadian poets, and story writers edited by D. G. Jones, Joseph Bonenfant, Richard Giguère and Sheila Fischman, was launched at the Université de Sherbrooke.

Prose translations have also become reasonably abundant in the sixties, with Philip Stratford, Glen Shortliffe, Jean Simard, Harry Binsse, Joyce Marshall, Derek Coltman, and Sheila Fischman among others, doing competent work. Felix Walter, who with Dorothea Walter produced an excellent rendition of Ringuet's *Trente Arpents* away back in 1940, continues to operate effectively. Translation, then, appears to be finally reaching something like a state of health, or perhaps I should say half a state of health. In both poetry and prose, unfortunately, translation has been in recent years preponderantly a one-way proposition—from

French to English. At the moment, Hugh MacLennan, Northrop Frye and Marshall McLuhan are the only English-Canadian creative writers whose book-length works are travelling the other way.

The cultural bridges created by competent translations, needless to say, can be of immense value to the development of Comparative Canadian Literature as a discipline. But more important, understandably, is the literary criticism which actually constitutes this field of study. Compared to translation, Canadian literary criticism focusing on works in French and English together has until the last few years been virtually non-existent. There have been occasional articles on individual authors of one language group written by persons of the other language group, such as Hugo MacPherson's essay "The Garden and the Cage" on Gabrielle Roy. Dorothy Duncan, the late wife of Hugh MacLennan, and A. Brown also wrote essays on Roy. "Roger Lemelin: The Pursuit of Grandeur," by W. E. Collin, appeared in *Queen's Quarterly* in 1954, and Collin's earlier *The White Savannahs* (1936) included a study of the French-born novelist Marie Le Franc, who spent long periods in Québec and set most of her work there. The writings of Marius Barbeau are the subject of an essay by E. MacMillan published in 1962.

Two general studies of French-Canadian literature have been around for several years: Jane M. Turnbull's *Essential Traits of French-Canadian Poetry* (1938) and Ian Fraser's *The Spirit of French Canada* (1939). Other enthusiastic bridge-builders were E. K. Brown, who included works in both languages when he introduced the "Letters in Canada" section of the *University of Toronto Quarterly* while he was editor of that periodical during the thirties, and B. K. Sandwell, who did translations and who prepared all the biographical and historical material on French-Canadian literature for Cassell's *Encyclopedia of Literature* (since revised and updated).

Probably the first critical comment in French on the
works of an English-speaking author of what is now
Canada appeared in 1841 in the *Revue des Deux
Mondes*. This long essay, written by a Philarète Chasles
on Thomas Chandler Haliburton, was quaintly entitled
"Samuel Slick." The same periodical brought out
another piece on Haliburton, "Un Humoriste Anglo-
Americain" by Emile Montégut, in 1850, but like the
reference to Haliburton as "the father of American
humour" in American literary histories, this essay did
not do much to advance the cause of Letters north of
the border. After a lean period of almost a century, "Où
l'encontre un Canadien," an appreciation of E. K.
Brown by Georges Bugnet, appeared in *Canadien-
Français* in 1946. More recently, the newspaper *Le
Devoir* has published short critiques on English-
Canadian authors, including Hugh MacLennan (by J.
Vallerand), E. J. Pratt (by Guy Sylvestre) and Irving
Layton (by Gilles Marcotte). Naïm Kattan, a man well
versed in many literatures, has written several general
surveys which have been printed in *Le Devoir*, in
Volume Two of *Archives des Lettres canadiennes*, and
in the magazine *Liberté*. It is of interest also to note
that Adrien Thério's useful annual review of literature
Livres et auteurs canadiens (now *Livres et auteurs
québécois*) for several years incorporated a short survey
by H. C. Campbell of works published by English-
speaking authors.

Slightly irrelevant to our purposes here perhaps, but
quite intriguing is the fact that in 1960 a certain Paul
Goetsch actually published a whole book in Hamburg,
Germany, resoundingly entitled *Das Romanwerk Hugh
MacLennan; eine Studie zum literarischen Nationalismus
in Kanada*. It is somewhat disheartening to consider
that as yet there is not one published book-length
critical study in French of an English-Canadian author

nor in English of a French-Canadian author.

The materials I have outlined above, of course, are not Comparative Canadian Literature, but simply some of the attempts which have been made to break through the culture barrier of Canada by increasing awareness of one side by the other. A little closer to actual comparative study are the literary histories of Camille Roy and Lorne Pierce. Roy's *Manuel d'histoire de la littérature canadienne-française*, first published in 1918, despite its title includes remarks on some English-Canadian authors. Lorne Pierce moved further towards an all-embracing attitude in his *An Outline of Canadian Literature* (1927) and the short biographical studies of his "Makers of Canadian Literature" series, which included Louis Fréchette, Antoine Gérin-Lajoie and François-Xavier Garneau along with nine English-language writers. Pierre, a man of broad and possibly prophetic vision, formulated the dream that the various cultures of Canada could be blended to distil something nationally inclusive and unique. He expounded this notion in a series of pamphlets—*Toward the Bonne Entente* (1929), *New History for Old* (1931), *The Armoury in our Halls* (1941), *A Canadian People* (1945) and *A Canadian Nation* (1960)—and it is perhaps the closest Canada as a nation has ever come to being offered a positive myth.

The absence of positive myths in both bodies of Canadian literature, incidentally, is the subject of another pioneering study—"Love and Death in Canadian Poetry," a thesis written for Carleton University, by Thomas E. Farley. It is a genuine pity that no Canadian publisher has yet undertaken to print this controversial thesis, for it contains many original and stimulating ideas. Edmund Wilson's *O Canada*, published in 1965, although highly selective and, being directed to non-Canadian readers, much burdened with background information on politics and history, also contains a number of original observations on Canadian writers in English and French. But Wilson's treatment of Canadian literature is more compartmental than comparative, touching only on what has caught the eye of an interested outside observer.

The essay which begins this volume, "Twin Solitudes," was a conscious attempt to examine Canadian writing in English and French taken together as a single national literature—in other words, Comparative Canadian Literature proper. It was delivered as an address at the annual meeting of the Learned Societies of Canada in June, 1966, and distributed in photocopies, then a few months later published in the periodical *Canadian Literature*. By the time the second essay, "The Body-Odour of Race," was also delivered as an address, to a combined group of students and professors at the "Second Century Week" held at Edmonton and Calgary in March of 1967, interest in the area of study had begun to expand. At that time, several students at Sherbrooke had embarked upon research for theses in Comparative Canadian Literature, and the following year two of these were completed. In 1969, *L'Age de la littérature canadienne* by Clément Moisan appeared. This book provided a general survey of selected writers and critics in both language groups, echoing some of the observations in "Twin Solitudes" and concluding with a strong endorsement of Comparative Canadian Literature as an inviting field of literary activity. And as the initiative taken at Sherbrooke gained outside recognition and approval, work continued on the inside. Also in 1969, Antoine Sirois, director of the French Department at the Université de Sherbrooke, brought out his *Montréal dans le roman canadien*, an exhaustive analysis of how the Canadian metropolis has figured in the fiction of writers of both language groups. D. G. Jones' *Butterfly on Rock*, published in 1970, purports to concentrate on anglophone writing, but in fact it offers insights into a number of French-Canadian works. Meanwhile, other essays included in this volume have appeared in literary journals, Antoine Sirois and Max Dorsinville have each contributed articles to *Canadian Literature*, more theses have been completed and new theses undertaken. It would appear that Comparative Canadian Literature has been safely launched as a fertile area of study and will continue to grow as Canadian writers themselves continue to grow—in quantity and quality, and because of comparative criticism, in awareness of each other.

166

End Notes

All references are to editions listed in the bibliography.

1. Tu mourras quand le bon Dieu voudra qu tu meures, et à mon idée ça n'est pas encore de ce temps icitte. Qu'est-ce qu'il ferait de toi? Le Paradis est plein de vieilles femmes, au lieu qu'icitte nous n'en avons qu'une et elle peut encore rendre des services, des fois. *(p. 193)*

2. Jésus-Christ, qui tendais les bras aux malheureux, pourquoi ne l'as-tu pas relevé de la neige avec tes mains pâles? Pourquoi, Sainte Vierge, ne l'avez-vous pas soutenu d'un geste miraculeux quand il a trébuché pour la dernière fois? Dans toutes les légions du ciel, pourquoi ne s'est-il pas trouvé un ange pour lui montrer le chemin? *(p. 146)*

3. Oh! la certitude! Le contentement d'une promesse auguste qui dissipe le brouillard redoutable de la mort! Pendant que le prêtre accomplissait les gestes consacrés et que son murmure se mêlait aux soupirs de la mourante, Samuel Chapdelaine et ses enfants priaient sans relever la tête, presque consolés, exempts de doute et d'inquiétude, sûrs que ce qui se passait là était un pacte conclu avec la divinité, qui faisait du Paradis bleu semé d'étoiles d'or un bien légitime. *(p. 218)*

4. "Peut-être qu'il oublie des fois. Il y a tant de misère qui s'adresse à lui." Ainsi, la seule fêlure dans sa foi venait de cette candide supposition que Dieu, distrait, fatigué, harassé comme elle, en arrivait à ne plus accorder qu'une attention éparse aux besoins humains. *(p. 89)*

5. Seulement faut pas s'aviser de réfléchir, de regarder, de soupçonner, de jouer à l'intellectuel. *(p. 98)*

6. Les croisements peuvent être un élément de progrès entre des races supérieures, assez voisines telles que les Anglais et les Allemands d'Amérique. Ils constituent toujours un élément de dégénérescence quand ces races, même supérieures, sont trop différentes.

   Croiser deux peuples, c'est changer du même coup aussi bien leur constitution physique que leur constitution mentale ... Les caractères ainsi restent au début très flottant et très faibles. Il faut toujours de longues accumulations héréditaires pour les fixer. Le premier effet des croisements entre des races différentes est de détruire l'âme de ces races, c'est-à-dire cet ensemble d'idées et de sentiments communs qui font la force des peuples et sans lesquels il n'y a ni nation ni patrie ... C'est donc avec raison que tous les peuples arrivés à un haut degré de civilisation ont soigneusement évité de se mêler à des étrangers. *(p. 131)*

7. Qui sait ... si notre ancienne noblesse canadienne n'a pas dû sa déchéance au mélange des sangs qu'elle a trop facilement accepté, trop souvent recherché? Certes, un psychologue eût trouvé le plus vif intérêt à observer leurs descendants. Ne vous paraît-il pas, mon ami, qu'il y a quelque chose de trouble, de follement anarchique, dans le passé de ces vieilles familles? Comment expliquez-vous le délire, le vertige avec lequel trop souvent les rejetons de ces nobles se sont jetés dans le déshonneur et dans la ruine? *(pp. 130-131)*

8. Lantagnac n'avait suivi que de loin l'éducation de ses fils et de ses filles. Chez eux il connaissait le fond, les qualités de tempérament; peu ou point la forme de l'esprit. Leurs succès l'ayant toujours rassuré sur leur dose d'intelligence, il s'était abstenu de pousser plus loin son enquête. Et maintenant voici qu'il découvrait ces deux surtout de ses élèves, il ne savait trop quelle imprécision maladive, quel désordre de la pensée, quelle incohérence de la personnalité intellectuelle: une sorte d'impuissance à suivre jusqu'au bout un raisonnement droit, à concentrer des impressions diverses, des idées légèrement complexes autour d'un point central. Il y avait en eux comme deux âmes, deux esprits en lutte et qui dominaient tour à tour. Fait étrange, ce dualisme mental se manifestait surtout en William et en Nellie, les

168

deux en qui s'affichait dominant le type bien caractérisé des
Fletcher. Tandis que Wolfred et Virginia accusaient presque
exclusivement des traits de race française: les traits fins et bronzés
des Lantagnac, l'équilibre de la conformation physique, en
revanche l'aînée des filles et le cadet des fils, tous deux de
chevelure et de teint blonds, plutôt élancés, quelque peu
filiformes, reproduisaient une ressemblance frappante avec leur
mère. *(p. 130)*

9 .   William, lui, restait toujours le même, esprit buté et bilieux. A
mesure que le cadet avançait en âge, les traits saxons s'accusaient
plus fortement dans la figure et par tout le corps du long
adolescent. La barre du front se faisait plus raide, la moue des
lèvres plus arrogante; presque toujours on le voyait s'en aller, la
nuque cambrée, les poings à demi-fermés, à l'allure d'un joueur de
rugby. *(p. 168)*

10 .   Je me souviens de t'en avoir parlé, Aaron. La seule condition
de survie: n'être plus Juif . . . Le Juif atteindra à tout, à condition
de n'être plus Juif . . . Alors nous . . . nous sommes Français, tu
vois? Mon père tire certaines ficelles pour que nous obtenions la
nationalité française. *(p. 143)*

11 .   Bérubé arracha fiévreusement sa vareuse, s'assit sur le lit pour
déboutonner sa chemise. Il tremblait: il avait la sensation que le
lit était chargé d'électricité . . . .
La fille était devant lui, nue. Elle avait gardé son soutien-gorge
rempli à se déchirer. Elle tendit les bras à Bérubé qui était
incapable de se lever, de bondir vers cette fille nue, de l'attraper
dans ses bras, de la serrer violemment, puis de la lancer sur le lit.
Bérubé se sentait complètement veule, comme lorsqu'il buvait
trop d'alcool. Dans sa tête, il entendait un tic-tac comme des
coups de tambour. "Toujours, jamais," répétait cette mon-
strueuse horloge, qui avait marqué les heures de son enfance,
l'horloge de l'enfer, qui durant toute l'éternité dit: "toujours
jamais": les damnés sont pour toujours en enfer, ils n'en
ressortent jamais: "Toujours, jamais." Sous l'horloge, Bérubé
voyait les visqueuses cavernes de l'enfer où rampaient les serpents
mêlés aux flammes éternelles, et il voyait les damnés nus étranglés
par les flammes et les serpents, "Toujours, jamais," scandait
l'horloge de son enfance, l'horloge de la damnation éternelle dont
souffrent ceux qui se mettent nus et ceux touchent à des femmes
nues, "toujours, jamais" sonnait l'horloge et Bérubé ne put
s'empêcher de supplier:
—Do you want to marry me?
—Yes, répondit la fille à qui on n'avait jamais posé cette
question.

—What's your name?
—Molly. *(pp. 37-38)*

12 .   Une certaine idée de Dieu, qui n'est pas Dieu, dit l'abbé
Savoie, mais sa plus subtile déformation, est ne moi comme une
plaie profonde, infligée et entretenue depuis trop longtemps pour
que je pervienne à la fermer. *(p. 217)*

13 .   Un soir, Hermann fit inviter Lucien et moi-même à un "wild
party" chez les Pinon. Qu'est-ce qu'un "wild party"? Une sorte
de ripaille à laquelle se livrent de petits clans de bourgeois, et où
l'on se laisse aller à tous les excès du manger, du boire et même de
l'amour. Ces noces communautaires ont lieu surtout à la fin de la
semaine, entre dix heures du soir, le samedi, et sept heures du
matin, le dimanche, alors que chacun s'en va à l'église, pour
effacer les péchés de la nuit. *(p. 98)*

14 .   On regarde, tout autour, comme si on cherchait. On regarde,
on regarde. On ne voit rien de bon. Si on fait attention quand on
regarde comme ça, on s'aperçoit que ce qu'on regarde nous fait
mal, qu'on est seul et qu'on a peur. On ne peut rien contre la
solitude et la peur. Rien ne peut aider. La faim et la soif ont leurs
pissenlits et leurs eaux de pluie. La solitude et la peur n'ont rien.
(p. 8)

15 .   Ma mère est comme un oiseau. Quand je la prenais dans mes
bras, elle se raidissait, elle se défendait. Reste tranquille! Va jouer
dehors! Tu me fais mal! C'est assez! ... Elle m'aime, mais d'une
curieuse façon ... Quand elle était assise dans les fleurs, j'allais
m'asseoir sur elle et la prenais par le cou. Va jouer comme une
bonne petite fille! Laisse maman tranquille! Maman est fatiguée!
Quand elle se promenait, je la suivais, je me pendais à sa robe. Elle
me laissait la suivre sans s'occuper de moi. Puis elle se retournait
et me disait qu'elle avait assez joué avec moi. *(p. 21)*

16 .   Tu peux regarder, si tu veux ... Ce n'est pas si grave! Un
Russe regarderait. Je ne comprends rien aux Canadiens. Regarde,
Christian. *(p. 65)*

17 .   Gloria est enterrée mardi. Je m'en tire avec les bras en écharpe.
Je leur ai menti. Je leur ai raconté que Gloria s'était d'elle-même
constituée mon bouclier vivant. Si vous ne me croyez pas,
demandez à tous quelle paire d'amies nous étions. Ils m'ont crue.
Justement, ils avaient besoin d'héroïnes. *(p. 282)*

18 .   Penchés de plus en plus au-dessus de notre petite nappe que le
poids de son eau creuse, nous sommes sur des charbons plus
ardents que si nous sassions des sables aurifères. L'eau puisée file
entre nos jambes, puis, se raréfiant, se met à goutter. Il n'en reste
plus qu'une soupe de plus en plus épaisse de limon et d'algues.

L'eau boueuse se met à bouger. L'eau boueuse s'anime, se met à bouillir. J'imagine, qui se dégagent des secousses de cette gestation insupportable, je ne sais quels pendants d'oreilles frétillants, je ne sais quelles minuscules fées à nageoires, je ne sais quelles fleurs vivantes de marguerite et de dahlia. Le fourmillement se précise, se peuple. Des dos luisent. Des queues surgissent. Je vois déjà grouiller la foule des petits têtards noirs. J'en attends d'autres, les gros, les pâles et tièdes comme des oeufs de moineaux, ceux dont la gorge est blanche et molle comme une joue, ceux qui poussent des pattes de bourdon à la racine de leur belle queue en fer de lance qui s'effrite. A côté des autres, ils ont l'air de géants, ils sont merveilleux, presque monstrueux. Ils emplissent le poing quand on les serre pour sentir la vie les travailler. Chaque fois, quand toute l'eau s'est vidée, une sorte de miracle s'est produit. Une sangsue grande comme un lacet a bondi, ondulant de toute sa longueur. Un vrai petit poisson d'aquarium, un petit poisson transparent luisant vert ou luisant bleu s'est dégagé de la masse des petits têtards noirs et des petits mollusques immobiles. *(pp. 35-36)*

19 . Le rabbi Schneider parle de ceux qui ne craignent pas le vrai Dieu. Il dit que le Dieu des Armées a dit qu'Il foudroiera ceux qui ne le craignent pas, qu'Il ne leur laissera ni racine ni feuillage. Si le rabbi Schneider pense que j'ai peur, il se fourre le doigt dans l'oeil. Les frissons qu'Il me donne, son "Dieu des Armées," ce sont des frissons de colère. Plus il en parle, plus je le méprise. Ils ont un Dieu comme eux, à leur image et à ressemblance, un Dieu qui ne peut s'empêcher de haïr, un Dieu qui grince des dents tellement sa haine le fait souffrir. Quand le rabbi Schneider parle comme ça, je pense à mon orme. Mon orme se dresse au milieu de notre grande île, seul comme un avion dans l'air. Ce doit être un impie. Je ne lui ai jamais vu de feuilles. Son écorce tombe en lambeaux; on peut la déchirer comme du papier. Sous l'écorce, c'est lisse lisse, doux doux. Quand il vente, ses grandes branches sèches claquent, on dirait qu'il est plein de squelettes. *(pp. 11-12)*

20 . Mon pays livré comme charogne, il y a plus de cent ans, à une bande de loyalistes à grandes dents. Mon pays bourré de soutanes multicolores, de petits épiciers, de maigres scieurs de bois, quelques géants isolés, exceptions qui entretiennent nos légendes, qu'un grand gaillard à l'air d'un castor chante à tue-tête à la face de nos collégiens boutonneux, de nos fonctionnaires cacochymes, de nos commis des coins de rue—il y a, au parlement, une bande de grosses morues, tous le nez au fond de gros fromages à taxes, taxes des "p'tits culs" épiciers et fonctionnaires, une armée de rongeurs, qui se font bénir tous les dimanches, qui paradent en

déclamant des âneries qui font des promesses. Ils se font élire sans peine en trompant le peuple, en débauchant les cervelles de nos épiciers-fonctionaires. En coulisses de ce théâtre de vermine, les soutanes et les loyalistes applaudissent. *(pp. 67-68)*

21 .   La campaigne qu'il faut mener. Tu sais, cette guerre, la vraie. Cette bataille pour terrasser cette grande vache grasse, ce veau malade et paresseux qui est couché sur nous. Sur ton pays et sur le mien. Sur le peuple noir, sur le peuple de la Grèce, sur celui de la Turquie et sur celui de la Chine et de l'Ecosse. Une grosse bête. Le mal, Ethel, le vrai mal, le seul, c'est l'ignorance. Voilà une bonne raison de se battre. C'est là le vrai ennemi. Notre seul ennemi. L'ignorance. Ethel, l'ignorance, rien n'est plus grave, ne plus mauvais. C'est elle qui sème les confusions, qui entretient la médiocrité, les tabous et les préjugés. *(pp. 113-114)*

22 .   Max Dorsinville, *Black Negroes and White Negroes: A Comparative Analysis of the Black American and French-Canadian Novel of Protest* (Thesis presented for Master of Arts Degree in Comparative Canadian Literature, Université de Sherbrooke, 1968). See also *"La Négritude et la littérature québécoise,"* *Canadian Literature*, No. 42 (Autumn, 1969). *(pp. 26-36)*

23 .   Il avait empoigné son Sten par la courroie, lui faisait faire un moulinet qui déchiqueta une branche d'arbre au-dessus de sa tête; il le rabattit dans la figure de son insulteur, que tomba foudroyé. Lanthier dirigea vers son ventre le canon du Sten et pressa la détente jusqu'à ce que le chargeur fût vide. L'Allemand sursauta, et, pendant quelques instants, fut agité d'une convulsion hideuse. Puis son corps se tordit comme celui d'un ver et s'immobilisa finalement. *(p. 143)*

24 .   A une heure, Richard donna un autre billet de $5.00 à la Minoune. Il avait oublié la guerre.
A deux heures, il lui donna un nouveau billet. Il avait oublié la guerre et l'après-guerre.
A trois heures, il lui donna le dernier billet qui restait dans son porte-feuille. Il avait oublié la guerre, l'après-guerre, la Vie, et lui-même. Quant à la Minoune, elle semblait avoir oublié le St. George Café. *(p. 250)*

25 .   For a full analysis of McDougall's *Execution* see my essay "The Vital Pretense," *Canadian Literature*, No. 27 (Winter, 1966), pp. 20-31.

Bibliography

The editions listed are the ones which I have used in preparing
this volume of essays, and to which all page references in the text
are made. Generally these editions are the most readily available.
The abbreviation NCL is for the New Canadian Library Series of
McClelland and Stewart Ltd., Toronto. See separate listing for
translations.

PRIMARY SOURCES:

Allister, William. *A Handful of Rice.* London: Secker & Warburg,
 1961.
Aquin, Hubert. *Prochain épisode.* Montreal: Cercle du Livre de
 France, 1965.
————. *Trou de mémoire.* Montreal: Cercle du Livre de
 France, 1968.
Aubert de Gaspé, Philippe. *Les anciens Canadiens.* Montreal,
 Fides, 1961.
Bacque, James. *The Lonely Ones.* Toronto: McClelland and
 Stewart, 1969.
Barbeau, Charles-Marius. *Le Rêve de Kamalmouk.* Montreal:
 Fides, 1948.
Beaulieu, Victor-Lévy. *Mémoires d'outre-tonneau.* Montreal:
 Editions Estérel, 1968.

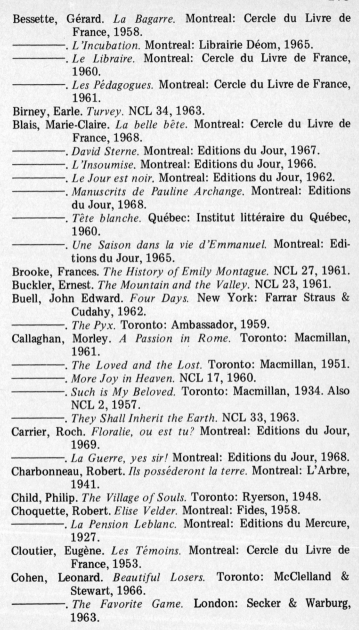

Bessette, Gérard. *La Bagarre.* Montreal: Cercle du Livre de France, 1958.

————. *L'Incubation.* Montreal: Librairie Déom, 1965.

————. *Le Libraire.* Montreal: Cercle du Livre de France, 1960.

————. *Les Pédagogues.* Montreal: Cercle du Livre de France, 1961.

Birney, Earle. *Turvey.* NCL 34, 1963.

Blais, Marie-Claire. *La belle bête.* Montreal: Cercle du Livre de France, 1968.

————. *David Sterne.* Montreal: Editions du Jour, 1967.

————. *L'Insoumise.* Montreal: Editions du Jour, 1966.

————. *Le Jour est noir.* Montreal: Editions du Jour, 1962.

————. *Manuscrits de Pauline Archange.* Montreal: Editions du Jour, 1968.

————. *Tête blanche.* Québec: Institut littéraire du Québec, 1960.

————. *Une Saison dans la vie d'Emmanuel.* Montreal: Editions du Jour, 1965.

Brooke, Frances. *The History of Emily Montague.* NCL 27, 1961.

Buckler, Ernest. *The Mountain and the Valley.* NCL 23, 1961.

Buell, John Edward. *Four Days.* New York: Farrar Straus & Cudahy, 1962.

————. *The Pyx.* Toronto: Ambassador, 1959.

Callaghan, Morley. *A Passion in Rome.* Toronto: Macmillan, 1961.

————. *The Loved and the Lost.* Toronto: Macmillan, 1951.

————. *More Joy in Heaven.* NCL 17, 1960.

————. *Such is My Beloved.* Toronto: Macmillan, 1934. Also NCL 2, 1957.

————. *They Shall Inherit the Earth.* NCL 33, 1963.

Carrier, Roch. *Floralie, ou est tu?* Montreal: Editions du Jour, 1969.

————. *La Guerre, yes sir!* Montreal: Editions du Jour, 1968.

Charbonneau, Robert. *Ils posséderont la terre.* Montreal: L'Arbre, 1941.

Child, Philip. *The Village of Souls.* Toronto: Ryerson, 1948.

Choquette, Robert. *Elise Velder.* Montreal: Fides, 1958.

————. *La Pension Leblanc.* Montreal: Editions du Mercure, 1927.

Cloutier, Eugène. *Les Témoins.* Montreal: Cercle du Livre de France, 1953.

Cohen, Leonard. *Beautiful Losers.* Toronto: McClelland & Stewart, 1966.

————. *The Favorite Game.* London: Secker & Warburg, 1963.

174

Conan, Laure. *Angéline de Montbrun*. Montreal: Fides, 1967.
Connor, Ralph. *The Man from Glengarry*. NCL 14, 1960.
Davies, Robertson. *A Mixture of Frailties*. Toronto: Macmillan, 1958.
—————. *Leaven of Malice*. Toronto: Clarke Irwin, 1954.
—————. *Tempest-tost*. Toronto: Clarke Irwin, 1950.
De la Roche, Mazo. *Delight*. NCL 21, 1961.
Desbiens, Jean-Paul (Frère Pierre Jérôme). *Les Insolences du Frère Untel*. Montreal: Editions de l'homme, 1960.
Desmarchais, Rex. *La Chesnaie*. Montreal: L'Arbre, 1942.
Ducharme, Réjean. *L'Avalée des avalés*. Paris: Gallimard, 1966.
—————. *Le Nez qui voque*. Paris: Gallimard, 1967.
—————. *L'Océantume*. Paris: Gallimard, 1968.
Duncan, Sara Jeannette. *The Imperialist*. NCL 20, 1961.
Elie, Robert. *La Fin des songes*. Montreal: Beauchemin, 1950.
—————. *Il suffit d'un jour*. Montreal: Beauchemin, 1957.
Fontaine, Robert. *The Happy Time*. New York: Dell, 1945.
France, Claire (pseudo. for Claire Morin). *Les Enfants qui s'aiment*. Montreal: Beauchemin, 1956.
Fréchette, Louis-Honoré. *Christmas in French Canada*. Toronto, 1899.
Garner, Hugh. *Cabbagetown*. Toronto: Ryerson Press, 1969.
—————. *The Silence on the Shore*. Toronto: McClelland & Stewart, 1962.
—————. *Storm Below*. Toronto: Ryerson Press, 1949.
Gérin-Lajoie, Antoine. *Jean Rivard*. Montreal: Beauchemin, 1953.
Girard, Rodolphe. *Marie Calumet*. Montreal: Editions Serge Brosseau, 1946.
Giroux, André. *Au delà des visages*. Montreal: Variétés, 1948.
—————. *Le Gouffre à toujours soif*. Québec: Institut littéraire du Québec, 1953.
Godbout, Jacques. *L'Aquarium*. Paris: Editions du Seuil, 1962.
—————. *Le Couteau sur la table*. Paris: Editions du Seuil, 1965.
—————. *Salut Galarneau!* Paris: Editions du Seuil, 1967.
Godfrey, Dave. *Death Goes Better with Coca Cola*. Toronto: House of Anansi, 1967.
Goulet, Robert. *The Violent Season*. New York: G. Braziller, 1961.
Graham, Angus. *Napoléon Tremblay*. Translated by André Champoux. Montreal: Beauchemin, 1945.
Graham, Gwethalyn. *Earth and High Heaven*. NCL 13, 1960.
Grandbois, Alain. *Né à Québec*. Paris: A. Messein, 1933.
Gravel, Pierre. *A Perte de Temps*. Toronto/Montreal: Anansi/Editions Parti Pris, 1969.

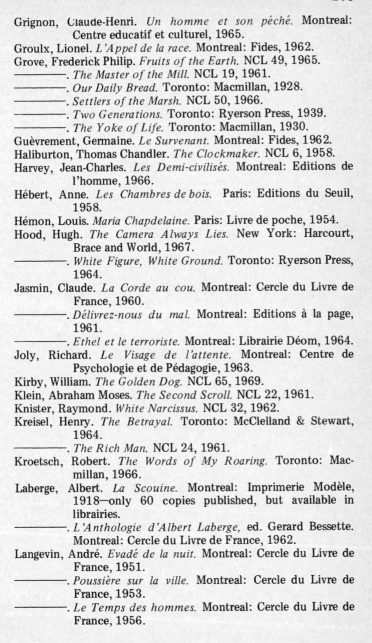

Grignon, Claude-Henri. *Un homme et son péché.* Montreal: Centre educatif et culturel, 1965.

Groulx, Lionel. *L'Appel de la race.* Montreal: Fides, 1962.

Grove, Frederick Philip. *Fruits of the Earth.* NCL 49, 1965.

————. *The Master of the Mill.* NCL 19, 1961.

————. *Our Daily Bread.* Toronto: Macmillan, 1928.

————. *Settlers of the Marsh.* NCL 50, 1966.

————. *Two Generations.* Toronto: Ryerson Press, 1939.

————. *The Yoke of Life.* Toronto: Macmillan, 1930.

Guèvrement, Germaine. *Le Survenant.* Montreal: Fides, 1962.

Haliburton, Thomas Chandler. *The Clockmaker.* NCL 6, 1958.

Harvey, Jean-Charles. *Les Demi-civilisés.* Montreal: Editions de l'homme, 1966.

Hébert, Anne. *Les Chambres de bois.* Paris: Editions du Seuil, 1958.

Hémon, Louis. *Maria Chapdelaine.* Paris: Livre de poche, 1954.

Hood, Hugh. *The Camera Always Lies.* New York: Harcourt, Brace and World, 1967.

————. *White Figure, White Ground.* Toronto: Ryerson Press, 1964.

Jasmin, Claude. *La Corde au cou.* Montreal: Cercle du Livre de France, 1960.

————. *Délivrez-nous du mal.* Montreal: Editions à la page, 1961.

————. *Ethel et le terroriste.* Montreal: Librairie Déom, 1964.

Joly, Richard. *Le Visage de l'attente.* Montreal: Centre de Psychologie et de Pédagogie, 1963.

Kirby, William. *The Golden Dog.* NCL 65, 1969.

Klein, Abraham Moses. *The Second Scroll.* NCL 22, 1961.

Knister, Raymond. *White Narcissus.* NCL 32, 1962.

Kreisel, Henry. *The Betrayal.* Toronto: McClelland & Stewart, 1964.

————. *The Rich Man.* NCL 24, 1961.

Kroetsch, Robert. *The Words of My Roaring.* Toronto: Macmillan, 1966.

Laberge, Albert. *La Scouine.* Montreal: Imprimerie Modèle, 1918—only 60 copies published, but available in librairies.

————. *L'Anthologie d'Albert Laberge,* ed. Gerard Bessette. Montreal: Cercle du Livre de France, 1962.

Langevin, André. *Evadé de la nuit.* Montreal: Cercle du Livre de France, 1951.

————. *Poussière sur la ville.* Montreal: Cercle du Livre de France, 1953.

————. *Le Temps des hommes.* Montreal: Cercle du Livre de France, 1956.

Laurence, Margaret. *A Jest of God.* Toronto: McClelland & Stewart, 1966.

——. *The Stone Angel.* NCL 59, 1965.

Le Franc, Marie. *La Randonnée passionnée.* Montreal: Fides, 1962.

Lemelin, Roger. *Au Pied de la pente douce.* Montreal: L'Arbre, 1948.

——. *Pierre le magnifique.* Paris: Flammarion, 1953.

——. *Les Plouffes.* Paris: Flammarion, 1955.

Le Pan, Douglas. *The Deserter.* Toronto: McClelland & Stewart, 1964.

Leprohon, Rosanna Eleanor. *The Manor House of Villerai.* Montreal: The Family Herald, 1859.

Lowry, Malcolm. *Ultramarine.* Philadelphia: Lippincott, 1962.

——. *Under the Volcano.* Harmondsworth, England: Penguin, 1962.

Ludwig, Jack. *Confusions.* Toronto: McClelland & Stewart, 1963.

MacLennan, Hugh. *Barometer Rising.* Toronto: Collins, 1941.

——. *Each Man's Son.* NCL 30, 1962.

——. *The Precipice.* Toronto: Collins, 1948.

——. *Return of the Sphinx.* Toronto: Macmillan, 1967.

——. *Two Solitudes.* Toronto: Collins, 1945.

——. *The Watch That Ends the Night.* Toronto: Macmillan, 1959.

Major, André. *Le Cabochon.* Montreal: Editions Parti Pris, 1964.

——. *La Chair de poule.* Montreal: Editions Parti Pris, 1965.

——. *Le Vent du diable.* Montreal: Editions du Jour, 1968.

Marcotte, Gilles. *Le Poids de Dieu.* Paris: Flammarion, 1962.

——. *Retour à Coolbrook.* Paris: Flammarion, 1965.

Marlyn, John. *Under the Ribs of Death.* NCL 41, 1964.

Martin, Claire. *Doux-amer.* Montreal: Cercle du Livre de France, 1960.

——. *Quand j'aurai payé ton visage.* Montreal: Cercle du Livre de France, 1962.

McCourt, Edward. *Fasting Friar.* Toronto: McClelland & Stewart, 1963.

——. *Walk Through the Valley.* Toronto: McClelland & Stewart, 1959.

McDougall, Colin. *Execution.* Toronto: Macmillan, 1958.

Mitchell, W. O. *Who Has Seen the Wind.* Toronto: Macmillan, 1947.

Moodie, Susanna. *Roughing It in the Bush.* Toronto: McClelland & Stewart, 1923. Also NCL 31.

Paradis, Suzanne. *Les Cormorans.* Québec: Librairie Garneau, 1968.

——. *François-les-oiseaux.* Québec: Librairie Garneau, 1967.

——. *Les hauts cris.* Paris: Editions de la Diaspora, 1960.

——. *Il ne faut pas sauver les hommes.* Québec: Garneau, 1961.

Pinsonneault, Jean-Paul. *Jérôme Aquin.* Montreal: Beauchemin, 1960.

Portal, Ellis (pseudo. of Bruce Power). *Killing Ground.* Toronto: Peter Martin Associates, 1968.

Renaud, Jacques. *Le Cassé.* Montreal: Editions Parti Pris, 1964.

Richard, Jean-Jules. *Neuf jours de haine.* Montreal: Cercle du Livre de France, 1968.

Richardson, John. *Wacousta.* NCL 58, 1965.

Richler, Mordecai. *The Apprenticeship of Duddy Kravitz.* NCL 66, 1969.

——. *Cocksure.* Toronto: McClelland & Stewart, 1968.

——. *The Incomparable Atuk.* Toronto: McClelland & Stewart, 1963.

——. *Son of a Smaller Hero.* NCL 45, 1966.

Ringuet (pseudo. of Philippe Panneton). *Trente Arpents.* Montreal: Fides, 1964.

Ross, Sinclair. *As For Me And My House.* NCL 4, 1957.

Roy, Gabrielle. *Alexandre Chênevert.* Montreal: Beauchemin, 1964.

——. *Bonheur d'occasion.* Montreal: Beauchemin, 1965.

——. *La Montagne secrète.* Montreal: Beauchemin, 1967.

——. *La petite poule d'eau.* Montreal: Beauchemin, 1964.

——. *Rue Deschambault.* Montreal: Beauchemin, 1964.

Ryga, George. *Ballad of a Stone Picker.* Toronto: Macmillan, 1966.

——. *Hungry Hills.* Toronto: Longmans, 1963.

Savard, Félix-Antoine. *Menaud, maître-draveur.* Montreal: Fides, 1966.

Sheldon, Michael. *The Personnel Man.* Toronto: McClelland & Stewart, 1966.

Simard, Jean. *Mon Fils pourtant heureux.* Montreal: Cercle du Livre de France, 1956.

——. *Les Sentiers de la nuit.* Montreal: Cercle du Livre de France, 1959.

Symons, Scott. *Place d'Armes.* Toronto: McClelland & Stewart, 1967.

Tardivel, Jules-Paul. *Pour la patrie.* Montreal: La Croix, 1936.

Thériault, Yves. *Aaron.* Montreal: Editions de l'homme, 1965.
──────. *La Fille laide.* Montreal: Beauchemin, 1950.
Thério, Adrien. *Soliloque en hommage à une femme.* Montreal: Cercle du Livre de France, 1968.
Vaillancourt, Jean. *Les Canadiens errants.* Montreal: Cercle du Livre de France, 1954.
Watson, Sheila, *The Double Hook.* Toronto: McClelland & Stewart, 1959. Also NCL 54.
Wilson, Ethel. *Swamp Angel.* NCL 29, 1962.
Wiseman, Adele. *The Sacrifice.* Toronto: Macmillan, 1956.

SECONDARY SOURCES:
Cox, Harvey. *The Secular City.* Harmondsworth, England: Pelican Books, 1968.
Dewart, Edward Hartley (ed.) *Selections from Canadian Poets.* Montreal: John Lovell, 1864.
Jones, Douglas Gordon. *Butterfly on Rock.* Toronto: University of Toronto Press, 1970.
Klinck, C. F., & Watters, R. E. (ed.) *Canadian Anthology.* Toronto: W. J. Gage, 1966.
Lorenz, Konrad. *On Aggression.* Translated by Marjorie Latzke. London: Methuen, 1966.
Marcotte, Gilles. *Une littérature qui se fait.* Montreal: H.M.H., 1962.
Moisan, Clément. *L'Age de la littérature canadienne.* Montreal: H.M.H., 1969.
Purdy, A. W. (ed.) *The New Romans – Candid Canadian Opinions of the United States.* Edmonton: M. C. Hurtig, 1968.
Sirois, Antoine. *Montréal dans le roman canadien.* Paris: Didier, 1969.
Wade, Mason. *The French-Canadian Outlook.* New York: Viking, 1946.
Weber, Max. *The Protestant Ethic and the Spirit of Capitalism.* New York: Charles Scribner's Sons, 1958.
Wilson, Edmund. *O Canada – An American's Notes on Canadian Culture.* London: Rupert Hart-Davis, 1967.

French-Canadian Fiction In English Translation:
Aquin, Hubert. *Prochain épisode – Prochain Episode* tr. Penny Williams. Toronto: McClelland & Stewart, 1967.
Aubert de Gaspé, Philippe. *Les anciens canadiens – The Canadians of Old* tr. G. M. Penée. Québec: Desbarats, 1864; *The Canadians of Old* tr. C. G. D. Roberts. New York: Appleton, 1890; *Seigneur d'Haberville* tr. Penée. Toronto: Musson, 1905; *Cameron of Lochiel* tr. Roberts. Boston: L. C. Page, 1927.

Barbeau, Marius. *Le Rêve de Kamalmouk—Mountain Cloud.*
Toronto: Macmillan, 1944.

Bessette, Gérard. *L'Incubation—Incubation* tr. Glen Shortliffe.
Toronto: Macmillan, 1967.

──────. *Le Libraire—Not For Every Eye* tr. Glen Shortliffe.
Toronto: Macmillan, 1962.

Blais, Marie-Claire. *La belle bête—Mad Shadows* tr. Merloyd
Lawrence. Toronto: McClelland & Stewart, 1960.

──────. *Le Jour est noir—The Day is Dark* tr. Derek Coltman.
New York: Farrar Straus & Giroux, 1967.

──────. *Tête blanche—Tête-Blanche* tr. Charles Fullman.
Toronto: McClelland & Stewart, 1961.

──────. *Une saison dans la vie d'Emmanuel—A Season in the
Life of Emmanuel* tr. Derek Coltman. New York:
Farrar Straus & Giroux, 1966.

Carrier, Roch. *La Guerre, yes sir!—La Guerre, yes sir* tr. Sheila
Fischman. Toronto: House of Anansi, 1970.

Conan, Laure. *A l'oeuvre et à l'épreuve—The Master Motive.* St.
Louis, Mo.: Herder, 1909.

Constantin-Weyer, Maurice. *La Bourrasque—The Half-Breed.* New
York: The Macaulay Co., 1930.

──────. *Un homme se penche sur son passé—A Man Scans His
Past.* Toronto: Macmillan, 1929.

Ducharme, Réjean. *L'Avalée des avalés—The Swallower Swallowed*
tr. Barbara Bray. London: Hamish Hamilton, 1968.

Elie, Robert. *La Fin des songes—Farewell My Dreams* tr. Irene
Coffin. Toronto: Ryerson, 1954.

France, Claire. *Les Enfants qui s'aiment—Children in Love* tr.
Antonia White. Toronto: McClelland & Stewart, 1959.

Giguère, Diane. *Le Temps des jeux—Innocence* tr. Peter Green.
Toronto: McClelland & Stewart, 1962.

──────. *L'Eau est profonde—Whirlpool* tr. Charles Fullman.
Toronto: McClelland & Stewart, 1966.

Godbout, Jacques. *Le Couteau sur la table—Knife on the Table*
tr. Penny Williams. Toronto: McClelland & Stewart,
1967.

Guèvremont, Germaine. *Le Survenant & Marie-Didace* combined—
The Outlander tr. Eric Sutton. New York: McGraw-
Hill, 1950; also under title *Monk's Reach.* London:
Evans Bros., 1950.

Harvey, Jean-Charles. *Les Demi-civilisés—Sackcloth for Banner* tr.
Lukin Barrette. Toronto: Macmillan, 1938.

Hébert, Jacques. *Les Ecoeurants—The Temple on the River* tr.
Gerald Taaffe. Montreal: Harvest House, 1967.

180

Hémon, Louis. *Maria Chapdelaine—Maria Chapdelaine* tr. W. H. Blake. Toronto: Macmillan, 1921; tr. Andrew MacPhail. Montreal: Chapman, 1921.

Jasmin, Claude. *Ethel et le terroriste—Ethel and the Terrorist* tr. David Walker. Montreal: Harvest House, 1965.

Langevin, André. *Poussière sur la ville—Dust Over the City* tr. John Latrebe and Robert Gottlieb. Toronto: McClelland & Stewart, 1955.

Le Franc, Marie. *Grand Louis l'innocent—The Whisper of a Name* tr. George and Hilda Shively. Indianapolis: Bobbs-Merrill, 1928.

Lemelin, Roger. *Au pied de la pente douce—The Town Below* tr. Samuel Putnam. New York: Reynal & Hitchcock, 1948; also NCL 26.

—————. *Pierre le magnifique—In Quest of Splendour* tr. Harry Lorne Binsse. Toronto: McClelland & Stewart, 1955.

—————. *Les Plouffes—The Plouffe Family* tr. Mary Finch. Toronto: McClelland & Stewart, 1950.

Marcotte, Gilles. *Le Poids de Dieu—The Burden of God* tr. Elizabeth Abbott. Toronto: Copp Clark, 1964.

Ringuet. *Trente Arpents—Thirty Acres* tr. Felix and Dorothea Walter. Toronto: Macmillan, 1940; also NCL 12.

Routhier, Adolphe-Basile. *Le Centurion—The Centurion.* St. Louis, Mo.: Herder, 1910.

Roy, Gabrielle. *Alexandre Chênevert—The Cashier* tr. Harry Lorne Binsse. Toronto: McClelland & Stewart, 1955; also NCL 40.

—————. *Bonheur d'occasion—The Tin Flute* tr. Hannah Josephson. Toronto: McClelland & Stewart, 1958; also NCL 5.

—————. *La Montagne secrète—The Hidden Mountain* tr. Harry Lorne Binsse. Toronto: McClelland & Stewart, 1962.

—————. *La petite poule d'eau—Where Nests the Water Hen* tr. Harry Lorne Binsse. New York: Harcourt Brace, 1951; also NCL 25.

—————. *La Route d'Altamont—The Road Past Altamont* tr. Joyce Marshall. Toronto: McClelland & Stewart, 1967.

—————. *Rue Deschambault—Street of Riches* tr. Harry Lorne Binsse. Toronto: McClelland & Stewart, 1957; also NCL 56.

Savard, Félix-Antoine. *Menaud, maître-draveur—Boss of the River.* Toronto: Ryerson, 1947.

Thériault, Yves. *Agaguk—Agaguk* tr. Miriam Chapin. Toronto: Ryerson, 1963.

—————. *Ashini—Ashini.* Toronto: Ryerson, 1964.

Vigneault, Gilles. *Contes sur la pointe des pieds – Tales on Tip Toe*
tr. Paul Allard. (part of thesis presented for Master of
Arts in Comparative Canadian Literature, Université
de Sherbrooke, 1969).

For a list of stories, poetry, drama, autobiography and belles-
lettres in translation, see Philip Stratford, "French-Canadian
Literature in Translation,"*Meta,* XIII, 4 (Decembre, 1968).

English-Canadian Fiction In French Translation:
Aside from nineteenth-century works such as William Kirby's *The
Golden Dog (Le Chien d'or* tr. Pamphile Lemay, 1884) and
Rosanna Leprohon's *The Manor House of Villerai (Le Manoir de
Villerai* tr. E. L. de Bellefeuille, 1861) and two novels by visitors
to Canada (Angus Graham's *Napoleon Tremblay – Napoléon
Tremblay* tr. André Champoux, 1945; Malcolm Lowry's *Under
the Volcano – Sous le volcan*), to my knowledge only five modern
Canadian novels have to date been translated from English into
French. They are Robert Goulet's *The Violent Season (Charivari),*
Gwethalyn Graham's *Earth and High Heaven,* and Hugh Mac-
Lennan's *Two Solitudes (Deux Solitudes* tr. Louise Gareau-des-
bois, Paris: Presse de l'Imprimerie moderne, 1963), *The Watch
That Ends the Night (Le Matin d'une longue nuit* tr. Jean Simard,
Montreal: Editions H.M.H., 1963) and *Barometer Rising (Le
Temps tournera au beau* tr. Jean Simard, Montreal: Editions
H.M.H., 1966).

INDEX